TESTIMC

DIRECT DELIBERᴀᴛɪᴠᴇ ᴅᴇᴍᴏᴄʀᴀᴄʏ
By
Debra Campbell and Jack Crittenden

"Democracy for the people and by the people. The reality too often falls far short of this ideal. Debra Campbell and Jack Crittenden argue powerfully in this fascinating new book for a direct deliberative democracy that challenges both our theories and practices of democracy. The public yearns to have its voice heard. This book makes the case for how. Start your dialogue today."

—Thom Brooks, Dean & Professor of Law and Government, Durham University (UK), author of *Becoming British: UK Citizenship Examined.*

"In this book Campbell and Crittenden present a powerful and demanding argument, one that forces anyone interested in democracy to consider the viability of approaches to truly genuine forms of direct participation."

—Gar Alperovitz, author of *America Beyond Capitalism* and Co-Chair of The Next System Project

"Oscar Wilde once remarked that socialism would never work. "It takes too many evenings." Genuine democracy – not façade democracy – suffers from the same failing. If we want a democracy, we are going to have to work at it. Campbell and Crittenden take that responsibility seriously, and in this extremely original book, they offer a proposal – legislative juries – designed to make democracy for the first time genuinely possible. Is their proposal perfect? Of course not. But is it worth thinking about, fighting for, trying, improving? The answer is Yes, if we are serious about the ideal that, on the 4th of July, we pretend to honor."

—Robert Paul Wolff, emeritus professor of philosophy, University of Massachusetts - Amherst, author of *In Defense of Anarchism*

In *3-D Politics: The Case for Direct Deliberative Democracy Now!* Debra Campbell and Jack Crittenden provide the most sustained and persuasive case for participatory democracy since Benjamin Barber's 1984 classic *Strong Democracy*. Wide-ranging in its philosophical, historical and empirical analysis, it provides an accessible and convincing defense of the idea that the people are capable of ruling themselves in a direct deliberative democracy. In these times of the rise of "populist" movements on both the left and the right, with their attendant hopes and fears, Campbell and Crittenden provide a timely reminder that a truly populist system is one in which average citizens are given the opportunities to participate in making at least some of the decisions that affect their lives. To instantiate these opportunities, they propose both deliberative democratic schools, and most uniquely, the incorporation of legislative juries composed of average citizens in the initiative process. The American system trusts and relies upon juries to make important decisions in the legal system; Campbell and Crittenden demonstrate why it should do the same on important political decisions as well. 3-D Politics would empower citizens, engage them in dialogue with fellow citizens on important political issues, and move the United States closer toward the democratic ideal.

—Dr. Michael Morrell, Associate Professor of Political Science, University of Connecticut, author of *Empathy and Democracy: Feeling, Thinking and Deliberation*

Direct Deliberative Democracy

HOW CITIZENS CAN RULE

DEBRA J. CAMPBELL

AND

JACK CRITTENDEN

BLACK ROSE BOOKS

Montréal • New York • Chicago • London

BLACK ROSE BOOKS No. TT394

Hardcover — ISBN: 978-1-55164-671-8
Paperback — ISBN: 978-1-55164-669-5
PDF — ISBN: 978-1-55164-673-2

Library and Archives Canada Cataloguing in Publication

Campbell, Debra J., author
    Direct deliberative democracy : how citizens can rule
/ Debra J. Campbell and Jack Crittenden.

ISBN 978-1-55164-669-5 (softcover).--ISBN 978-1-55164-671-8
(hardcover).--ISBN 978-1-55164-673-2 (PDF)

    1. Deliberative democracy. I. Crittenden, Jack, author   II. Title.

JC423.C36 2018   321.8   C2018-902117-9
                                       C2018-902118-7

CP. 35788 Succ. Léo-Pariseau,
Montréal, QC, H2X 0A4
CANADA
www.blackrosebooks.com

ORDERING INFORMATION

USA/INTERNATIONAL	CANADA	UK/EUROPE
University of Chicago Press	University of Toronto Press	Central Books
Chicago Distribution Center	5201 Dufferin Street	Freshwater Road
11030 South Langley Avenue	Toronto, ON	Dagenham
Chicago IL 60628	M3H 5T8	RM8 1RX
(800) 621-2736 (USA) (773) 702-7000 (International)	1-800-565-9523	+44 (0) 20 852 8800
orders@press.uchicago.edu	utpbooks@utpress.utoronto.ca	contactus@centralbooks.com

Black Rose Books is the publishing project of Cercle Noir et Rouge.

TABLE OF CONTENTS

INTRODUCTION

Direct Deliberative Democracy... Why Not?

In 2000 David Broder, the Pulitzer-Prize winning columnist for *The Washington Post*, published his last book, *Democracy Derailed*. Around that same time, Debra had been researching the literature on initiatives, including the latest empirical studies, for her dissertation. When Debra read Broder's book, she discovered that virtually everything Broder wrote about initiatives and their pernicious effects on our democracy was refuted by the empirical data. Many of the assertions made in his book were just wrong. Broder, of course, was a highly regarded columnist. What he said about initiatives and about democracy carried weight, immense weight, with the book-reading public. Agitated by this discovery, and worried about the damage that Broder's misguided arguments might have, Debra came to talk with me (her dissertation Chair) about collaborating on writing a new book that would point out the flaws in Broder's arguments. I immediately agreed.

Our arguments, it turned out, went well beyond Broder's misunderstanding, and Debra's "legislative juries," her proposed remedy to Broder's misunderstandings, form the heart of our book.

We disagree with Broder's contention that citizens should not be directly involved in making laws (such as in the initiative process, a form of direct democracy) and that law-making should be exclusively in the hands of elected representatives. Part of Broder's reasoning involves his view that citizens cannot responsibly make laws. We asked ourselves, "Why can't we?" After much deliberation, we arrived at a simple answer: We can, and we should. This book tells how and why.

In his 1970 book, political philosopher Robert Paul Wolff asked his own question about direct democracy: "Why are we still relying on representatives to make the laws for us?" His answer was to install instantaneous direct democracy and to install it *now*. Even in 1970, long before the explosive power of the Internet, Wolff argued that America had the electronic means to allow all Americans to vote directly on public laws instead of just voting on candidates.

Today we certainly have the technology to carry out Wolff's vision. The current instantaneous availability of information eliminates two of the Founding Fathers' most compelling reasons for the necessity of representative government: the amount of time needed for disseminating information and the difficulty of communicating effectively over long distances. Both reasons are now moot.

Forty years later, with his book in its third edition, Wolff's summary is still compelling: All representative government of whatever sort is a compromise with the ideal of autonomous self-rule. If we are going to be self-governing, or autonomous, then a person can be bound only by a law that she participates directly in creating and adopting. To Wolff, even if you support a law, that law is still illegitimate for you because you didn't help to create it. As Jean-Jacques Rousseau reminds us, the public's reliance on representatives to make laws is not much better than "voluntary self-enslavement." The only way to be truly free, Rousseau contends, is to lay down the law for oneself.

Clearly not many people agree with Wolff and Rousseau; otherwise, we would have direct democracy by now. And if people did agree, then following Wolff we would have direct democracy in an extreme form. But surely it is no compromise of your autonomy if laws are passed without your vote or consent about the salary of librarians in Vermont, when you don't live in Vermont, work in Vermont, or serve as a librarian in Vermont. So there are many examples of laws that we didn't vote for that do not lessen our sense of autonomy. But the absence of participation on creating laws that do affect your life or work can be a movement against or away from autonomy.

We shall have much more to say in Chapter Four about autonomy and the legitimacy of laws, but for now it's important to understand that we are not suggesting that representative democracy has no place and should be abolished. Some issues like military retaliation for an immediate attack require a quick response and cannot await public input. There are cases where we agree to give authority to certain elected officials and to those with high levels of expertise—for example, addressing trade deficits or international treaties and agreements.

Instead, we are suggesting that certain forms of direct democracy enhanced by the power of deliberation should be more widely used as a complement to representative democracy. With the exception of the New England "town meeting" style of local governance, little direct democracy is practiced in America. Because representative democracy is the dominant form of democracy today, there is rarely any debate about whether we need representatives to make our laws for us. Rather, most arguments expressing concerns about representation are about *how* representation should be achieved, not about *whether* representation is necessary. Since direct democracy has not been much practiced in America until the recent upsurge in voter initiatives, contemporary theorists do not argue against direct democracy; rather, they rely on arguments from earlier centuries, arguments that we take up in the first two chapters.

On the other hand, the dramatic increase in the number of ballot initiatives over the past 30 years shows a movement toward more direct legislation by citizens (or direct democracy) in various states across the country. Since the current technology can support almost instantaneous information and online voting, then we might ask why only an elite group of citizens or "representatives" is able to sponsor all legislation. Why not have citizens simply propose and vote directly on legislation itself? Or to pose the question from a different direction, what is wrong with initiatives? Why should we oppose this form of direct democracy?

Since the ratification of the U. S. Constitution on March 4, 1789, we have seen movements in America toward more democracy. For example, by the beginning of the twentieth century the constitutional method of *appointing* senators had come to be viewed by most Americans as undemocratic. The Seventeenth Amendment (ratified in 1913) rejected the appointment of senators and allowed for senators to be chosen by popular election.

Perhaps the time has come for a new compromise. Just as there was the "great compromise" over how representation was to take place when the U.S. Congress was first formed—by population (in the House of Representatives) or by strict equality (in the Senate)—we may need another compromise, one between direct and representative democracy. Though we may still need state and federal legislators to enact some laws, such as laws about foreign policy and how to structure the national debt, other laws may be formulated by a form of direct democracy—the initiative process—bolstered by what we term "legislative juries."

For us, the key to citizens making laws is not simply empowering them to do so through direct democracy, but also to assure that citizens make laws through deliberation in the kind of examination of arguments and evidence that courtroom juries do. This will entail citizens of all sorts working in small groups—multiple small groups—deliberating on the social, political, and economic policies important in their lives. Thus, we envision juries, legislative juries. Such juries are the centerpiece of our arguments in this book. From our perspective direct democracy requires a level of deliberation. Otherwise, we have only plebiscitary democracy in which all citizens have to do is show up or push a button, irrespective of how little they know about the proposed law or bill. This is one way that we strongly differ from the proposal of Robert Paul Wolff.

We believe that we desperately need a democracy that lives up to its literal definition of "people rule" (*demos kratia*). What we currently have in the United States and around the world is not literal democracy, and what we want is real democracy—"people power."

Now everyone *claims* to want democracy, because it signifies that each person will have some say and more control over his or her life. As Winston Churchill once observed, democracy is the worst form of government, except for all the others. So everyone wants democracy for herself or himself. What they aren't sure about is whether their neighbors and the people they see at the DMV should have a say in the government. People joke that they are all for dictatorship as long as they are the dictators. The joke is not far removed, or far enough removed, from concerns about democracy. "I can handle the power," many seem to say, "but I'm not sure about the Clancys down the street who think that *Star Trek* is a documentary about space travel and who barbecue using a welder's torch."

The wealthy throughout history have worried that if the poor and the undereducated had political power, they would strip the rich of their property and use it to enrich themselves. Thus many national leaders, including our own Founding Fathers, established property qualifications for voting. They ensured that the wealthy would have more power than the poor. But in the Athens of Pericles, in the home of the first democracy, the penniless citizens were equal participants with the wealthiest. All could participate equally in the Assembly that deliberated and passed laws. The Athenians certainly incorporated a level of deliberation in their decision-making in the form of open debate.

But if we aren't sure about our neighbors having democracy, then maybe we aren't ready for it ourselves. Because democracy means that all citizens are able to participate actively and equally with all others. Yet participation as we envision it is not simply voting. In our view democracy is more than that, more demanding than that. Built in must be the requirement for citizens to deliberate with one another. Deliberation makes all the difference, as we discuss at length in the following chapters, because it calls on participants to exercise the capacities that we all have but are underutilized or totally ignored in our current system.

Of course, it seems ironic that while some people worry that more direct democracy (making our own damn laws) will have too many people (of the wrong sort?) participating, there is often the complaint that Americans today are apathetic and not likely to become involved in politics. So, the concern seems to be that if we have direct deliberative democracy, then too few people will be involved. Is that a problem? We say, "okay." Let those who want to participate have the opportunity to do so. Those who want to stay home, can. But we also think that democracy now will actually bring out more people, more citizens, to participate actively to direct their social and political lives. They don't do so currently because the system is, well, underwhelming.

To convey our emphasis on the deliberative nature of our version of direct democracy we considered calling our book "3-D Politics: Direct Deliberative Democracy."

So we dove into the 3-D angle: something that is 3-D has width, height, and depth. Most of us are well familiar with this concept, because our physical world is three-dimensional, and we negotiate it pretty well most of the time. In short, 3-D is reality, and if we want our politics to be real, then we want them to be 3-D: direct and deliberative and democratic. We want to see that our political decisions are wide, comprehensive and encompassing. We want to see that they have height—that they are significant in our lives and affect us directly and importantly. Finally, we want those decisions to have depth; we want them to have real substance and quality behind them. We want them made sensibly, reasonably, through dialogue and deliberation. So we want and need our democracy to be "real." We want and need it to be three-dimensional.

Then we began to think that perhaps "3-D Politics," though clever, is too abstract and that the reader doesn't really get to the democracy part until the subtitle, and by then you may have been stymied by the combination of "direct" and "deliberative." So we considered a different title: "Engaging Democracy." This would, similarly, have been a play on words. We want people to participate in our democratic system. We want people to "engage" in thinking about democracy, and more important, to actually "engage" in democratic processes to take control of their collective lives. Participation is one form of what is often called more generally "civic engagement." But in order to accomplish this, we must make our democracy more *engaging;* that is, more interesting to the people. What is the best way to get citizens to engage in their democracy? How do we encourage citizens to participate actively, to take a role in democracy? That is, how do we motivate citizens toward actively "engaging democracy?" Well, we must make our democracy more engaging.

This is a problem: The democratic system currently on offer to our citizens is not appealing. Congressional races are virtually predetermined, as incumbents win their seats nine out of ten times. Incumbents have an advantage because they can raise more money than their opponents, and this was true before the Supreme Court cases *Citizens United* and *McCutcheon*.[1] Also, lobbyists are eager to fill the incumbents' campaign war chests with the cash that buys those lobbyists access, if not favored treatment.[2] That access is seen not so much in buying a representative's vote outright; rather, it is seen in influencing who writes the bills and how they are written. Lobbyists spend money so that they can have a say, or a hand, in crafting any legislation related to their interests.

A polite way to describe this election mechanism is to say that the system is "skewed" in favor of those already in office and those with money. Because both political·parties benefit in the same way, though maybe not to the same extent, a less polite way to describe this is to say that the system is "rigged." Our citizens are asked really only to vote for or against some rascal...with another rascal waiting in the wings. This is the problem with the political view expressed often in democracies: If citizens dislike their elected representatives, then they can vote the rascals out. But in virtually all well-established representative democracies there is a line of rich and well-connected fresh-faced rascals waiting to get into the game. There is always such a line, because elected politics is where the power and money and influence are. But power should belong to the people. Otherwise, there is no democracy, no real democracy. Thus, the more citizens can participate directly in making laws, the less influence money can have and the more power the people can exert themselves.

Bear in mind, as we shall discuss in more depth, that our Founders had no intention of creating a democracy. As we all know from our schooling, they were wise men. In their wisdom they created a constitution for a sprawling nation, a nation that could be or could become a republic. That republic was never intended to be a democracy, though some elements were democratic for the minority—white, property-owning, males. But the democratic element was *intended* to be a minority aspect—that is, a small piece of the governing pie. The larger or largest piece was to be held by those of property. It wasn't quite as simple as "the more property one has, the more political power one wields," but look how things have turned out: Do those who contribute, and contribute mightily, to campaigns have greater access to and influence over politicians than common citizens and non-contributors?

It turns out that empirical evidence shows that those who contribute mightily to campaigns do have greater influence over politicians than common citizens and small-time contributors do. In their 2014 article, "Testing Theories of American Politics: Elites, Interest Group, and Average Citizens," Martin Gilens and Benjamin Page compiled data from roughly 1,800 policy initiatives between 1981 and 2002. They found through the data that lawmakers followed the directives of the 10 percent wealthiest Americans and followed the opinions of major lobbying and business groups. Moreover, lawmakers, according to the data, did not follow the directives of average Americans—those at the 50th percentile of income. In short, lawmakers respond to the policy demands of wealthy individuals and moneyed business interests, those with the most lobbying clout and deepest pockets for bankrolling campaigns. This situation is so dire that Gilens and Page conclude that "the preferences of the average American appear to have *only a minuscule, near zero, statistically non-significant impact* upon public policy" (emphasis added). Is this not direct evidence that the political system is skewed, if not rigged?

The Founders said the right things: political power comes from the consent of the governed. Really? When did you consent to having nuclear arsenals or to the welfare system? To gargantuan military budgets? To farm subsidies? To tax cuts for the wealthy? For insurance companies to run the healthcare system?

Did the Founders lay out a democracy that in reality has kept the pocket of democratic power quite small? Isn't that now what we see with corporations and unions and interests of all sorts gaining access to and influence over our "elected" politicians, especially since *Citizens United* and *McCutcheon*? Even worse, today the oligarchs themselves are in power as real-estate mogul Donald Trump occupies the White House with a Cabinet of corporate executives.

The Founders *did* create a democracy, or at least recognized democracy as the foundation of the republic. Notice that the Constitution's Preamble begins, "We the people…;" it does not begin, "We the 39 men in Philadelphia…." Power does reside in and does emanate from the people; the Founders acknowledged that. But the Founders simply assumed, as our leaders today assume, that the people would be focused on creating personal wealth more than on paying attention to politics. Many Americans today are too distracted by working and shopping and consuming and American dreaming to care much about exerting their political democratic power.

But the instruments of exercising that power are in place and in our hands. We simply need to awaken to what is already ours, and use it.

Many or most of those instruments are easily recognizable: the power of voting folks in and out of office, the use of pressure through those very same interest groups of which you are or might become a member, the use of the media to shine a bright light on the goings-on in Washington and in boardrooms, and the use of meetings (town halls, rallies, the Internet) to hold officials accountable. But we don't use those instruments or use them often enough. Some of them seem boring (town meetings) or useless (media) or corrupt and rife with hidden agendas (interest groups). Regardless of one's attitude, our attitude is that these instruments are not enough.

Now one can pretend that what CEOs, generals, and senators do has nothing to do with his/her immediate life. But as things turn out, that "nothing" is really "everything." As the source of political power, we, fellow citizens, are sovereign. That means everything done is done in our name. It has to be. If we are sovereign, then we rule ourselves. So if you like what your government, at whatever level, is doing, then get out there and use your power to reinforce the policy. If you don't like what the government is doing, then get out there and use your power to oppose the policy. If most of the time you don't care, then do nothing. But our sense is that the more we act on the policies that really matter, the more we shall find that policies about more and more issues matter more and more. And the more we act in politics as it is right now, the more we'll find that we can and should be doing even more. That "even more" is direct deliberative democracy.

So we want citizen engagement but only in a democratic system that is itself engaging. We are not interested in ways to increase voter turnout in our current system that is empty, sterile, lifeless, and rigged. *Engaging* democracy means developing a new democratic vision and encouraging and preparing citizens to engage in it by adopting this vision, working for it, working on it, and working in it.

At any given time in our democracy, but especially around elections, one can hear liberals and progressives arguing that it is time for citizens to take back their democracy, and we hear conservatives chanting "take America back!" Fine sentiments... even inspirational. But one cannot take back what one has never had. America's democratic system has never been in the hands of the people, has never been a product of the people, and, indeed, has never been "of the people" or "by the people." Our nation was founded as a republic in order to avoid its being or becoming a real democracy. What was true at the end of the eighteenth century is true as well early in the twenty-first.

So, from our perspective, we argue that direct democracy in some form is really what democracy *is*. True democracy is not a representative system. Representation makes our system some form of a republic with democratic trim. Therefore if we want democracy, real democracy, then we must have direct democracy. If we want direct democracy, then we need to be prudent about what forms that should take. We argue that the best form of democracy is direct deliberative democracy in the form of deliberative bodies, especially legislative juries. Thus the central piece, the cornerstone, of our book is legislative juries. These juries rest on the simple idea that people, ordinary folks, can think for themselves, can apply that thinking to governing themselves, and can do so immediately and well.

We went back-and-forth with our titles. One we tried, "Why Can't We Make Our Own Damn Laws?" struck the right chord, an insistent one, but it packed no punch without the "damn" in there, which we didn't really want to use. We liked the play-on-concept in "3-D Politics: The Case For Direct Deliberative Democracy," but the reader doesn't get to the point, as said, until after the colon. We also worried that rather than attracting readers to wonder what 3-D politics was about, the title might instead distract and, worse, confuse prospective readers. In short, would the title entice the reader or just provide an excuse to ignore the book?

Fortunately for us, expertise sprung from experience saved us from endless dithering. Our wise and merciful publishers, Black Rose Books, put us out of our misery by deciding for us. "Get to the point," they advised. "Tell the reader what the book is about." Hence the title *Direct Deliberative Democracy*.

Yet still enamoured of the idea behind 3-D politics, we decided to stick with that when we started our institute and website devoted to direct deliberative democracy: http://www.3-dpolitics.com/. We like to think of this book as an elaborate mission statement, even a manifesto, for the work that we shall do there.

No one should misunderstand what we mean when we say that we need democracy today. We are not promoting just any kind of democracy, not an extension or reformation of our current representative system and not a form of plebiscite where citizens can vote on anything at anytime for any reason and on any whim…and with no input or perspectives from others. We are calling for direct democracy where citizens make laws but do so through processes that include the requirement of deliberation. The political condition of requiring deliberation makes all the difference, since, as we argue in the book, it follows from years of experiments in social psychology. And so, for the well-being of our citizens and for the health of the nation, we argue that we need direct deliberative democracy.

Now it is time for you to begin your part for real democracy and read why we should deliberate with fellow citizens, with workplace associates, and with organization members to make our own damn rules and laws!

CHAPTER ONE

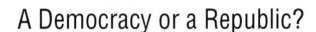

A Democracy or a Republic?

Why are many people opposed to direct democracy; that is, to having people create and vote directly on legislation that affects them? To answer that question many people refer to objections like those raised by the philosopher Plato in his famous political treatise, The *Republic*. Yet that answer raises another question: why would people dredge up the arguments of a philosopher who has been dead for over 2,000 years? Well, as Alfred North Whitehead once observed, all of Western philosophy can be understood as a series of footnotes to Plato (424 – 348 B.C.E.). If one considers that most American adults would likely recognize Plato's name, even without having read a word of his philosophy, Whitehead's remark should be taken seriously. Assuming that there is at least some truth to his claim, it is understandable that many people still rely on Plato's characterization and criticisms of democracy.

Plato's concerns about democracy are outlined in Book VIII of the *Republic*. He makes what many believe is a knock-down argument against direct democracy by arguing that people will rule only in their own self-interest and not in the interest of the common good; in other words, direct democracy would result in nothing but "mob rule." Furthermore, if Will Rogers' claim, "All I know is what I read in the papers" is likewise the truth for millions of Americans (although today we might substitute "television" or "media" for "newspapers"), then democracy may be in serious trouble because we can be influenced too easily by clever slogans and one-minute sound bites. So, in order to examine such concerns about direct democracy we can go all the way back to Plato and ancient Greece. Ancient Greece exemplifies the first and most pure form of direct democracy, and Plato's writings are most often cited as reasons that citizens should not vote directly on the making of laws.

While we examine the concerns surrounding direct democracy, we must also note that the terms "democracy" and "republic" are often used loosely and require some clarification. To understand governance in America today we have to be able to differentiate these two terms. The fact that these terms have evolved over time has caused people to confuse both the meanings of the two terms and what they mean for our government. While most Americans identify their government as both a "democracy" and a "republic," those same Americans, if asked, would be hard-pressed to explain the distinguishing features of either term. For example, we shall argue in the chapter on initiatives that David Broder in his book *Democracy Derailed* conflates republicanism and democracy when he criticizes the initiative process and claims that voting directly on legislation through initiatives is a "derailment" of democracy. This is particularly ironic, since initiatives are an actual practice of direct democracy, where people are voting directly on legislation rather than just voting for candidates. Thus, initiatives are much more democratic. So let us examine the terms "democracy" and "republic" and how such concerns as Plato's about "democracy" led the Founding Fathers to embrace a "republic" instead.

The Terms and Concerns: Democracy

As noted in the Introduction, the English word "democracy" is derived from the Greek words *demos* and *kratia* and quite literally means "rule (*kratia*) by the people (*demos*)." The democracy of some of the ancient Greek city-states, especially Athens, in the fifth century B.C.E. was "direct" democracy, in which all of the citizens could gather to vote directly on laws proposed by the citizens themselves. To be a citizen one had to be a free male over the age of 18 and had to have enough wealth and free time to participate. Thus "citizens" in ancient Athens were a very limited part of the population and did not include women, children, foreign workers, or slaves. Given the small geographic size of Athens and the limited number of citizens, participation was active and direct. There was no need to have someone else "representing" one's interests in this democracy.

In Athens, all the citizens could attend the *ekklesia*, or assembly. To carry out the business of governing, the *ekklesia* earlier met in the Agora, or marketplace, and then later met on the hillside of the Pnyx. Most historians estimate that there were about 43,000 citizens in the golden age of Athens, although the total population of Athens around this time was estimated to be between 250,000 and 275,000, or more than five times the number of citizens.[3]

Furthermore, until the reforms of Pericles in early 451-452 B.C.E only those citizens wealthy enough to spend time away from home or business would have been able to participate on a regular basis. One of those reforms allowed citizens payment for some kinds of participation, such as serving on juries. So, while the total number of citizens in Athens averaged from between 30,000 to 50,000 people, it is estimated that around 5,000 to 6,000 people might participate on any given day. Out of those 5,000, sufficient numbers were selected by lottery to serve on the juries, sit on the law-making councils, and vote on any other business of the day. The assembly was responsible for declaring war, determining military strategy, and electing other officials. It originally met once every month, but later it met three or four times per month. Mogens Herman Hansen in his book *The Athenian Democracy in the Age of Demosthenes* tells us that a quorum of 6,000 citizens was required for important votes, and that juries consisted of anywhere from 201 to 1,500 citizens chosen from any of the 6,000 attending on that day. The number of jurors impaneled depended on the type of case (civil or criminal) and how much money was involved in the dispute. The large number of jurors was intended to avoid corruption and bribery. In fact, if it were a very important case, all 6,000 citizens might serve on the jury. Votes were taken by a show of hands or by casting stones. Citizens dropped white stones for "yes" and black stones for "no" into large clay pots.

Thus, in its earliest incarnation, democracy was in the form of direct democracy, in which all Athenian citizens were entitled to attend the assembly and participate in the making of laws and in the administration of the city. In fact, participation was seen as a citizen's civic duty and essential to being a virtuous person. Notice how different this sounds from today, when people regularly try to wriggle out of jury duty when called to serve.

Plato's most famous student, Aristotle (384 – 322 B.C.E.), in his work, the *Politics*, gives an even more detailed description of democracy in early Athens. Aristotle outlined the characteristics of Athenian democracy in the following way. First, Greek democracy was widespread. Every citizen was eligible to be elected to those offices that they were subject to, such as tax collector, for example. However, quite often citizens were chosen to fill an office by having their names drawn in a simple lottery. There were generally no property qualifications for running for or holding office, though in those instances where there was any such qualification it was very low. Offices were rotated so that no one would hold office twice in a row, or certainly no more than twice.[4]

Thus, every citizen ruled at some point, or could, and was at the same time subject to the very laws that the citizens passed. In addition, citizens served on juries to sit in judgment on all matters pertaining to the city, ranging from grand matters, such as the nature and scope of the constitution, to business matters, such as making and enforcing private contracts. Thus, the assembly of citizens presided over all matters of the state.

Aristotle's description also tells us that democracy, in large part, was based on the principle of justice—that all citizens count and count equally—with neither the poor nor the rich counting for more than the other. Today we would describe this principle as "one person, one vote.".

Furthermore, in the democracy of Aristotle's time participation in the government was seen as important to fostering virtue in the citizenry. In ancient Athens, one could not be a good person if one were not a good citizen. To be a good person, one had to practice being a citizen by participating in governing. Aristotle argues in the *Nicomachean Ethics* that the development of virtue comes from the practice of good, or virtuous, activity until such practice becomes a habit.[5] So, the more one practiced being a good citizen—through participation in the affairs of the state— the more virtuous one would become. Imagine how different contemporary society might be if we thought that participating in politics increased our virtue?

Some of the more important features of Athenian democracy were that all citizens should serve on juries and attend law making assemblies, that citizens should be selected for political office by lottery, that citizens should not serve in the same position over and over, and that all citizens should count equally. Plato believed that such equality and freedom led to some serious problems. In the following, Plato describes how democracy unravels because of the excesses of too much freedom. Almost 2,400 years ago, Plato wrote:

> I mean that a father accustoms himself to behave like a child and fear his sons, while the son behaves like a father, feeling neither shame nor fear in front of his parents, in order to be free. A resident alien or a foreign visitor is made equal to a citizen, and he is their equal…A teacher in such a community is afraid of his students and flatters them, while the students despise

their teachers or tutors. And, in general, the young imitate their elders and compete with them in word and deed, while the old stoop to the level of the young and are full of play and pleasantry, imitating the young for fear of appearing disagreeable and authoritarian.[6]

Because of such "excesses," Plato goes on to state that the people lack the will and the education to be good rulers.[7] These uneducated masses do not understand the "good" in the sense of the *common good*, which is the goal toward which government should aim. According to Plato, most citizens lack both the knowledge and the virtue necessary to formulate just laws. Plato theorizes that whenever the *demos* attempts to govern itself, the society eventually becomes disorganized, and ultimately the people leave themselves open to the rise of a tyrant who takes over in an effort to restore order. So, Plato argues that democracies always devolve into tyranny, the form of government where one man rules in his own interest. Of course, a tyrannical government really is no better, since a tyrant always rules according to his own personal interests, and, therefore, the common good is still absent. Thus, Plato's main criticism about democracy is really a concern about where it ultimately can or might lead rather than a criticism of how it was practiced during the Golden Age of Athens (roughly 457 – 431 B.C.E.).

Though Plato makes some interesting predictions about the "excesses" of democracy that might seem relevant today, using Plato's vision of democracy as a source for criticism of direct democracy is relying on a very weak analogy. Those who rely on Plato's description of democracy to make the case against direct democracy in America today are forgetting about the clear differences that exist between the demographics and the democracy—as it was practiced—in ancient Athens and the demographics and the democracy—as it could be practiced—in America today.

Plato believed that, although citizens in a democracy enjoy the utmost freedom, the following bad consequences would occur: no one would want to rule, there would be competing constitutions (that people may or may not follow), and self-appointed leaders would pursue leadership positions mostly for their own interests. This characterization of democracy bears so little resemblance to the limited "democracy" present in the United States today that to continue to use Plato's concerns as the basis for criticisms against direct democracy now is like arguing to get rid of all cell phones because the earliest mobile phones weighed approximately five pounds and cost $3,995.00.

The differences between Plato's vision of democracy and democracy as it is understood and practiced in America today should be fairly obvious. First, in America there has been one constitution with relatively few amendments for over two hundred years; American democracy has not been subjected to "many constitutions." Second, there is no shortage of people who want to rule; many people today covet political power. The one concern of Plato's that still seems relevant is that our elected leaders may participate for their own self-interests and not for the common good. Whether elected leaders rule only in their own interest is open to debate; however, returning to the people the power to make legislation could help answer this concern.

To continue with the more general claim that Plato's criticisms are not applicable, there are other obvious dissimilarities between the citizenry of Plato's Athens and the citizenry of today's United States. For example, in the U.S. today more of the adult population are educated and enfranchised than at any other time in history. Given the broader inclusiveness in the citizenry and the broader distribution of wealth, we (at least for now) have in the United States a large, relatively stable middle class (although that does seem to be in jeopardy).[7] Since Plato's Athens had a large slave population, and women were not included in the citizenry, the dissimilarities are clear. Recall that around the time of 431 B.C.E., the total population of Athens averaged between 250,000-275,000. Of this number only between 30,000 and 50,000 (less than 20 percent) were citizens. The citizenry in Athens was limited to adult males who had the appropriate birthright, likely owned property, and had some education. In comparison, today in America, according to the 2010 U.S. Census, out of a total adult population of 308,745,538, over 87% have at least a high school education, and over 67% percent of the citizenry own their own homes. Thus, the proportion of propertied, educated citizens is much greater in the U.S. than in Plato's Athens.

The combination of over one hundred years of public education and the development of a stable middle class in the U.S. has manifested a democratic republic dramatically different from the tiny pocket of democracy of ancient Athens. In fact, the dissimilarities are so striking and obvious that one wonders why we would still compare the two. Is it even reasonable to think that democracy in America today would be anything like the democracy practiced in ancient Athens? So, is it reasonable to remain prejudiced against a contemporary version of direct democracy because of how it was practiced over 2,400 years ago in a population that was less than one percent the size of the U.S. today and had strikingly different demographics? It makes no sense to keep making the argument that there cannot be direct democracy in America today because it was short-lived in Athens over two millennia ago. However, although concerns like Plato's seem so outdated today, such arguments did convince America's Founding Fathers that "democracy" should be avoided and that the new American government should be a "republic" instead. To understand the movement from a "democracy" to a "republic" we need to move several hundred years forward from ancient Athens to Rome.

The Terms and Concerns: Republic

The term "republic" is derived from the Latin *res publica*, which literally means "things public." In Rome, the democratic element of republicanism was based on an active citizenry. Similar to Athens, participation in government was considered crucial to being a virtuous person. So republicanism like democracy involved the political participation of free citizens and the notion that political participation promoted virtue. As in ancient Athens, not all Romans were citizens, but there were various levels of citizenry. For example, free men over the age of 18 were full citizens; free women over the age of 18 were also citizens, but in a very limited sense. These women had some rights as free persons, but they could not vote or participate in government. Slaves, of course, were not citizens, although if they attained freedom, then they attained some limited rights.

The citizens of the Roman Republic were expected to put aside personal interests and to think about the common good when participating in politics. But instead of every citizen voting on every law, as in direct democracy, the republican tradition involved elements such as a "mixed" constitution, including the appointment of senators to carry out the making of laws. A "mixed" constitution or "mixed" government meant that some issues were decided by the majority of the people, while other tasks might be carried out by a particular elected or appointed official or group of people, like the senators. Thus, the republicanism of Rome contained elements of at least two different types of government: oligarchy (rule by a few, as in the elected or appointed senators), and democracy (rule by the many, as in people chosen by lot from all citizens). This mixture of governing is thought to be the precursor to the "separation of powers" guaranteed in the American government today.

In addition to the notions of virtue and active participation that characterize democracy, republicanism also included another aspect of "mixed government" inasmuch as no single class or group of people would rule. Another important aspect of the republicanism of Rome was the emphasis on the "rule of law," not of men. All citizens could participate in the making of the laws and all citizens were subject to the same laws. No "man" was above the law.

Much later in France, Jean-Jacques Rousseau continued much of this evolving republican tradition, but Rousseau emphasized the *direct* nature of democracy (harkening back to the democracy of Athens) and reaffirmed that a republic involved the citizenry's active participation in making the laws. This duty could not be assigned to representatives. According to Rousseau, the *active* part of citizenry cannot be delegated or alienated. Rousseau thought that being bound by laws that one did not vote for was akin to "voluntary, self-enslavement." Thus, handing over one's responsibility in the making of laws to a "representative" was in effect relinquishing one's freedom.

Rousseau believed that his ideal of all citizens participating equally in the making of the laws could take place only in a small venue where all citizens could meet to vote and create laws. Thus, a republic based on direct democracy would most likely be confined to a limited population in a small geographic area. In addition, Rousseau argued that all citizens would have to own some property in order to ensure their continued interest and participation in achieving the common good. If some citizens owned property and some did not, then inequities would result. For example, those who owned property might not want a "property" tax levied, whereas those who did not own property might think that such a tax would help fund public education, thereby ensuring the common good. In order to avoid such conflict in a democracy, Rousseau theorized that all citizens should own at least some property.

As the Founding Fathers imagined a new US Constitution, they wrestled with the problem of how to govern such a huge geographical expanse. Given that the elements of both direct democracy and those of a republic worked best only in a small geographic area, the Founding Fathers of the American republic were faced with no small task. How could the new nation hope to embrace democratic and republican ideals, particularly the active participation of the citizenry, in a territory the size of America?

James Madison attempted to provide an answer to that question in *Federalist #10*. The first part of Madison's solution involved turning away from the "democracy" that had been short-lived in both in Athens and Rome. Concerning such "democracies", Madison wrote:

> Hence it is that such democracies have ever been spectacles of turbulence and contention; have ever been found incompatible with personal security or the rights of property; and have in general been as short in their lives as they have been violent in their deaths.[8]

The second part of Madison's solution was to embrace instead a republic, but with an important modification. Madison re-defined the concept of a republic when he argued that representation was an essential component of a strong republic. In #10, Madison claims,

> A republic, by which I mean a government in which the scheme of representation takes place, opens a different prospect and promises the cure for which we are seeking.[9]

Madison contended that there were major differences between a democracy and a republic. In a republic, governing is delegated to a small number of citizens or representatives who are elected by the rest. In addition, a republic with such a large, diverse population extending over such a huge territory would naturally control the problem of factions. In other words, the vastness and diversity of America would ensure that no one group would become too powerful.

Madison argued that while the practice of representation was by definition non-democratic, it was necessary in order for a republic to survive in such a large nation-state. Delegating the responsibility for governing to select representatives is a significant break from the democratic and republican traditions of the ancients. According to the Greeks and Romans, the primary goal of government was to create virtuous people. Citizens could practice being virtuous by putting their immediate self-interest aside while attempting to create legislation aimed at the common good. Even through the time of Rousseau, an important element of a republic was the goal of creating good citizens. Such creation involves the *active* participation of citizens in politics. Thus delegating the making of laws to a small portion of the citizenry means that the majority of citizens will lack the opportunity to develop civic virtue, thereby making the creation of a virtuous citizenry impossible.

Of course, the Founders' movement away from the ancient Athenian type of direct democracy was not just a result of their reaction to the demise of Greece and Rome. The Founding Fathers were also heavily influenced by the most prominent political treatises of their day, including Thomas Hobbes' *Leviathan* and John Locke's *Second Treatise of Government*. Hobbes argued that men's self-interest would result in a war of "each against all." Therefore, government was needed to ensure a civil society and to keep the peace. Locke argued for the necessity of the consent of the governed and of a separation of powers within the government. Locke believed that the goal of civil society should be the protection of life, liberty, health, and possessions.

Together, these two ideas about the goal of government represented another important shift in the notion of republicanism; that is, the notion that the goal of civil society is the protection of individual rights to life, liberty, and property. Thus, the Founding Fathers embraced the idea that the purpose of government is to protect the rights of self-interested individuals. Madison followed this reasoning when he argued that the propensity of individuals to be self-interested meant that only men of a certain virtue, who could put their self-interest aside and rule for the common good, should make the laws and "represent" the interests of the people. Instead of politics creating virtuous people (as the ancient Greeks believed), Madison argued that politics should be practiced only by men who were already virtuous. Yet since most men lacked virtue, governing should be left in the hands of a small, select group of "fit" men.

Madison contended that in an extensive republic the protection of the rights of individuals would be accomplished best by representative democracy. The features of the new American "republicanism" debated during the Founding of America included the following:

1. Representative Democracy (instead of Direct Democracy)
2. Separation of Powers (Executive, Legislative & Judicial Branches)
3. Mixed Government (House of Representatives, Senate, and President—a mixture of rule by the many, the few, and the one)

Notice that the element of active citizenry was reduced to representation, where citizens voted only for candidates and not directly on legislation. Madison argued that the legislative function of the American republic needed to be handled by representatives elected to create the laws for the society as a whole. This view is an important step away from direct democracy; i.e., away from citizens' direct involvement in making of laws. In addition to believing that the vast size of the new republic resulted in the need for representation, Madison argued that factions and lack of virtue also made representative democracy (or republicanism) preferable to direct democracy.

Madison shifts our understanding of democracy away from the direct democratic form of ancient Athens, thereby rendering Plato's criticisms obsolete. However, Madison's concerns about democracy may themselves be obsolete. Of course, in order to give Madison's concerns the respect they deserve, we briefly examine the three arguments Madison gave for representative democracy as an improvement on the (in his view) impractical notion of direct democracy or direct involvement in the people making the laws.

Following Plato and Aristotle, Madison believed that the people—the poor, uneducated masses—were not fit to govern. There were three major problems with (direct) democracy: factions, tyranny of the majority, and the size of the geographic area to be governed. Madison argued that, conveniently, the answer to all three of these problems would be to elect representatives to make the laws for the rest of us.

Madison's first argument for representation rested on the problem of factions. Madison believed that a large and diverse population would result in various groups of people dividing up into factions based on similar interests. *Federalist #10* begins:

> Among the numerous advantages promised by a well-constructed Union, none deserves to be more accurately developed than its tendency to break and control the violence of faction.[10]

By "faction" Madison refers to a group of citizens constituting a majority or minority whose passion or interest is contrary or adverse to the rights of other citizens. According to Madison, evidence of factions abound:

> Complaints are everywhere heard from our most considerate and virtuous citizens, equally the friends of public and private faith and of public and personal liberty, that our governments are too unstable, that the public good is disregarded in the conflicts of rival parties, and that measures are too often decided, not according to the rules of justice and the rights of the minor party, but by the superior force of an interested and overbearing majority.[11]

Madison claims that in a pure democracy, such as that of ancient Athens, there is no solution to the problem of factions. However, factions did not lead to the downfall of Athens, nor were they one of the concerns mentioned by Plato. Nevertheless, Madison argues that there are only two ways to avoid the causes of factions: either eliminate liberty or give to all citizens the same opinions. Because either would be impossible, the effects of factions may be mitigated by electing representatives to create the laws. Thus, Madison's first argument for representation may be summarized as follows:

1. Factions cause divisiveness and are therefore a danger to the republic.
2. There are two ways to resolve the problem of factions— remove the causes or control their effects.

3. We cannot eliminate the causes of factions.
4. We can mitigate the effects of factions by replacing pure democracy with a representative republic.
5. Therefore, we need a representative republic.

There are a number of problems with this argument. First, premise three is false. In the opening pages of *Federalist #10*, Madison argues that the two causes of factions—liberty and differing opinions—make their elimination impossible. He assumes that democracy can work only when everyone shares the same views. Because the *causes* of factions cannot be overcome, the best way to avoid the *effects* of factions is to avoid pure democracy and replace it with a representative republic.

Since there is no way to remove the causes of factions, Madison moves on to premise four: controlling the *effects* of factions. However, Madison admits that one of the primary causes of factions, which heretofore he had omitted, is an unequal distribution of property. Madison adds to his argument as follows:

> The most common and durable source of factions has been the various and unequal distribution of property. Those who hold and those who are without property have ever formed distinct interests in society. Those who are creditors, and those who are debtors, fall under a like discrimination. A landed interest, a manufacturing interest, a mercantile interest, a moneyed interest, with many lesser interests, group of necessity in civilized nations, and divide them into different classes, actuated by different sentiments and views. The regulation of these various and interfering interests form the principal task of modern legislation and involves the spirit of party and faction in the necessary and ordinary operations of government.[12]

So, in addition to the two causes of factions already discussed, Madison cites a "most common" source of factions: the unequal distribution of property. Again, Madison sees no way to avoid this cause of faction, other than to leave the making of the laws to a few select men elected to represent all citizens' interests.

As a way to avoid this "most common and durable source of factions," both Aristotle and Rousseau argued that a more even distribution of property was necessary to a stable government. But Madison rejects this notion because the attendant loss of liberty would be too great. Ironically, many have argued that it is the American ideal of "home ownership" that has helped create such a large middle class. The large, relatively stable middle class in America affirms Aristotle's view of property as conducive to avoiding factions.

Nevertheless, not only did Madison ignore Aristotle's and Rousseau's cautions about the unequal distribution of property, but he also ignored some of his own contemporaries who had made this same point. The Anti-Federalists made a similar point when they argued in the famous "Centinel" essays that a free government can only exist where property is equally divided, a point to which we shall recur in the next chapter.

Today, over 67% of Americans own their own homes. In addition, the public goods and services that result from our system of taxation contributes to a large, relatively stable middle class. This, in turn, helps ease one of the causes of factions. Therefore, it is less clear what role representation, *per se*, plays in mitigating this cause of factions and renders Madison's argument less compelling.

The problem of factions is Madison's first argument for representation. The second argument rests on a concern known as "the tyranny of the majority" and is as follows:

1. In pure democracy there is a tendency for the majority to tyrannize the minority.
2. Tyranny of the majority ignores the rights of the minority and must be fought against.
3. One way to protect against a tyranny of the majority is to elect representatives to rule in terms of the public good.
4. Therefore, we need a representative republic.

However, this argument contains "the fallacy of missing the point;" that is, drawing a conclusion that is not really the most obvious conclusion. What is overlooked in this argument is that a better way to mitigate the oppression of minority interests is by constructing a strong constitution that defines a set of fundamental rights. Some Federalists and most Anti-Federalists understood that a strong Bill of Rights was a step toward mitigating the tyranny of the majority, and Madison eventually came to accept this conclusion. In a letter from James Madison to Thomas Jefferson dated October 17, 1788, Madison claimed that he had always been in favor of a bill of rights, so long as those rights were limited to only what was enumerated.[13]

Even though Madison argued that representation would help to prevent a tyranny of those in the majority, he also supported the Bill of Rights as a way to protect minority interests. Perhaps Madison did concede that representation, *per se*, was neither necessary nor sufficient for solving the problem of the majority oppressing those in the minority. In a later chapter we will mention again the "tyranny of the majority" problem and propose that empaneling impartial juries to make laws is another way we could mitigate that problem.

After acknowledging his concern about the "tyranny of the majority," Madison identified another related problem. Given Madison's belief that all men are, by nature, self-interested, how can representatives, acting as trustees and empowered to make all the laws, avoid falling prey to their own self-interests? In fact, if you begin with the premise that "men are by nature self-interested," it is difficult to see how anyone would conclude in favor of representative government because then one would be asking someone who *is* self-interested to represent *others'* interests. To relegate one's interests to someone else who is *self*-interested seems paradoxical. We shall recur as well to this topic in the next chapter, as we find Madison's answer to this concern—that we must select a few men of "fit character" to make the laws for us—severely lacking.

Madison's third argument for the necessity of representation was that many citizens, because of the size of the territory, would be unable physically to meet to deliberate and vote on laws. Madison argued that pure democracy must be confined to a small territory. Given the size of the United States and the difficulties surrounding transportation and communication, the laws would need to be formed by men selected to represent the views of the wider population. Thus, Madison's third argument for representation is as follows:

1. The size of the republic is too large for direct democracy, because people cannot readily assemble.
2. Electing representatives will solve this problem.
3. Therefore, we need a representative republic.

However, it does not follow that there be a selection of a few men "whose wisdom may best discern the true interest of their country." The American republic may have needed a representative system because of the problems of distance and travel. However, there was no argument that the representatives be chosen from a "select few" or that they be largely responsible for making all the laws. Indeed, Thomas Jefferson had another idea, which is detailed in Chapter 2, for how to accomplish this that involved all citizens directly in making the laws.

Given the speed with which information can now be disseminated, and the power of electronic voting, the response to Madison's third argument of "size" is that today "size" truly does *not* matter. Comparing the problems of democracy from ancient Athens and from eighteenth-century America with the problems of democracy today is similar to comparing the problems of computers from the 1950s with the problems of computers today.

In this book we propose that "direct democracy" be understood as the process whereby laws are created, proposed, and voted upon directly by the citizens, as opposed to the current practice of representative democracy, wherein laws are formulated, introduced, and voted on by elected representatives.

The preceding passages demonstrate that Madison's three arguments in favor of a representative republic formed the basis of the main concerns *against* pure or direct democracy. This abandonment of pure democracy has continued effortlessly from the formation of our republic to the present day, as described in the next chapter.

CHAPTER TWO

Democracy in Earlier America

The Founding

On the opening day of the Federal Convention, what we now call the Constitutional Convention, May 25th, 1787, Edmund Randolph, then governor of Virginia, took the floor. Randolph outlined to the gathered delegates Virginia's plan for a new constitution. Drafted by James Madison, the plan revealed that Virginia, at least, did not want simply to tinker with or fine-tune the Articles of Confederation, the document that joined the colonies into a confederation of independent, sovereign states. Instead, Randolph, speaking for Virginia, proposed a new federal constitution, because the Articles themselves were unable to thwart democracy. America's greatest danger, Randolph warned, was having too much democracy, which could be remedied, he continued, with a strong Senate elected by members of the House of Representatives and not by the people.

Randolph's warning is important, not because it went unheeded and America today has too much democracy, but because it has too little…and it always has. The warning provides a glimpse into the attitude of many of the delegates toward democracy, which is perhaps best summed up by Alexander Hamilton: "The voice of the people is said to be the voice of God…and it is not true in fact. The people are turbulent and changing, they seldom judge or determine right." Political power, Hamilton thought, should go to the rich and wellborn and not to the people.

Though they might not have agreed unanimously with Hamilton, the Founders focused their attentions, as we have seen, on establishing a republic, not a democracy. They concentrated, that is, on opposition to monarchy and in favor of representative government. In the place of any form of direct democracy the Founders wanted to establish a representative government so that all authority derived through representation from the people.

The Founders understood democracy to mean direct decision-making by the people themselves, as in ancient Athens and as Rousseau recommended. But in the cases both of Athens and Rousseau, the setting for democracy was always a small city-state. For a land as vast and diverse as the 13 colonies, such a political system seemed impractical. Yet practicality was not the only concern. In the eyes of many of the Founders, the quality of the people themselves raised serious questions about their abilities to make sound judgments.

Elbridge Gerry of Massachusetts feared democracy because, as he put it, "the people do not want virtue, but are the dupes of pretended patriots." The "people" are led into baseless opinions through "the false reports circulated by designing men."[14] The people, lacking virtue and, apparently, critical thinking, would now and always be misled by demagogues and scoundrels.

Of course, this fear of the manipulation of the people by "designing men" led most of the Founders to conclude that sound political decisions could be made only by the wealthy and wellborn; men precisely like Hamilton and most of the Founders themselves. Not one of those 55 men at the Constitutional Convention were about to create a democracy. The only "democratic" aspect of the newly formed government would be that the people—the citizens—would elect the representatives who would make their laws. Thus the average citizen's participation in their own governance would be limited to voting to elect the members of the House of Representatives.

Although the Founders were willing to have the people directly elect representatives to the House, they did so on the condition that the Senate, as Washington is alleged to have said to Jefferson, would be the saucer to cool the hot tea—that is, the cool deliberative body that would offset the possible democratic excesses that might flow from the House. Senators would be immune to the manipulations of rabble-rousers, rogues, and opportunists. As Randolph had suggested on the first day of the convention, they would be elected by the state legislators. These legislators would elect, the Founders hoped, the very best among them.

The task of the Founders seemed to be to *limit* power to the people. First, the people could not directly elect the President; that election will be done through state-appointed representatives to the Electoral College. Second, the people would not elect senators. Third, the people would elect only federal representatives, who will themselves mostly be the cream skimmed from the top of the state legislatures and from around the states. And the Senate will be able to override—even ride roughshod over—the House. Fourth, excluded from the ranks of "citizens" were children, of course, and those most like children: women and slaves. This practice harkened back to Aristotle and the view, held historically from the ancient world into the 20th century, that women and minorities somehow lacked the deliberative capacity to make good, independent decisions. Finally, the Founders established property qualifications. They feared that without such a provision, the poor would sell their votes to the rich or, worse from the Founders' perspective, the poor would vote themselves in and seize everyone's land. But if that were the worry, then shouldn't officeholders be restricted to those of wealth? Otherwise, those elected are open to bribery from lobbyists. That seems logical… and a complaint that is sadly still all too common.

Indeed, to the Founders all of these reasons seemed logical: The territory was too vast for a democracy and the people were not fit to rule. For the Founders so much depended on the character of the persons elected to office. They had to be men of fit character, men of merit and integrity. If the best men (those elected to the state legislatures) selected as Senators the best among themselves (those most prominent in their states), then would not the fit character of the decision-makers be all but guaranteed?

Money was not a criterion for office, not for the Founders. Character was. Madison thought that because there were so few seats in the federal government, the people would at least have sense enough to elect prominent citizens and civic leaders to those few seats. There weren't enough seats for the elite *and* the rabble or the selfish.

This meant for the Founders that the people themselves could not wield political power, as they were likely to be easily misled. But they could select men better than themselves to represent them; the people had virtue enough for that. Besides, having only to elect men to office meant that most people could then focus on what they preferred—making money. Indeed, it was the interest in commerce and money making that made the people unsuitable for office, because they would forever favor their own interests and profits and, lacking the vision of impartiality and evenhandedness characteristic of better men, they would always be incapable of or disinclined to look out for the common good.

So where were these men of fit character, these "better" men, to be found? In what occupations or areas of life? Not surprisingly, they were found among the landed gentry and within the learned professions. The Founders thought these men would be free from petty squabbling and obsessions with money. Such men could and would pursue what was best for the whole society, not just what was good for them as individuals or as a group.

But the Founders also knew that while such men might not pursue their own selfish interests, they still had them.[15] It would be impossible to keep sectional and factional interests out of politics altogether. Men would still argue for their interests and their friends' interests. The hope of the Founders was that such men might well start with such interests, but as men of character, they would not end there.

The genius of the American Constitution, then, was to offset one faction by another faction, which these fit representatives would do. We saw the genesis of this in the discussion of Madison's arguments for a representative democratic republic. That is, factions would cancel one another out so that no private or local interests would dominate the business of the federal government. There would be so many competing interests and groups within this vast territory—this "extended republic"—that no single interest or voice could dominate the majority.

In other words, these men of integrity or fit character would quickly see that there was little point in holding out for their own interests or that of their groups. Those interests and groups could not sway or dominate the majority; there would be too many groups and interests for that. Therefore, they would neutralize one another. The only sensible recourse, then, was to promote what was good for everyone, for the whole society or community.[16]

In addition, the separation of powers assured that this kind of competition extended among the branches and levels of government. In short, governing America would not rest, as in classical republicanism, on virtue and honor. It would rest on distrust: The states, not trusting the federal government, would balance that government; the federal government, not trusting the states, would check those states. The House of Representatives, not trusting the Senate, would check the Senate; the Senate, not trusting the House, would balance the House; the executive branch, not trusting the legislature, would check the legislative branch; the House and Senate, not trusting the President, would balance the White House. Perhaps "trust" is not quite the right word. The issue was one of susceptibility—which level or branch of government was most susceptible to corruption and tyranny?

Another part of the genius of the American Constitution was not only the recognition that the people were capable of selecting good men as representatives, but also the recognition that the people were *equally* capable of this. In most states the property qualifications for participating in elections were quite low; all the better to bring more people, but still the "right" people—the stakeholders with some property and thus something "at stake"— into the process. And this system of electing officials meant that everyone's vote counted equally. The vote of the backwoodsman was equal to that of the Boston lawyer or the Philadelphia printer. No one's vote counted for more than that of any other voter. This was one of the few democratic elements remaining from the democracy of ancient Athens.

The Founders thus created a system of electoral politics that would tap the people's capacities but not stretch them beyond their limits. The people were seen as having little political capacity beyond mere voting and voting only for candidates of a certain sort—men of fit character. Initially, the system worked just about as the Founders imagined it. Elected to the federal seats were, indeed, many prominent citizens and local notables. Elected, largely but not exclusively, were the patriotic or Revolutionary elite, those men who had directed the Revolution and, as a result, reaped the benefits of the people's thanks.

But there were also problems, even early on. Those elected even to the first Congress seemed to be representing very little but themselves and their own interests. In addition, with no hereditary nobility, with no aristocratic class, money rather than rank came to define who was "best," who was "fit."[17]

Of course, there were bribes, subtle and overt; there was horse-trading and you-scratch-my-back-and-I'll-fill-your-pockets-with-money. Only persons (or, in this case, men) of the right character could resist such temptations. This is precisely what Madison and the Founders had in mind. But with the fading of the Revolutionary cadre and with the influx of money as a factor in determining who was of fit character, thoughts soon turned to electing the new notables—the moneyed and property elite.

So who was elected? It seemed no one but the rich. The Anti-Federalists thought from the start that this would be the case.[18] They argued that there was no impartial valorous elite from which to draw candidates. There were only well-known men who had narrow interests of their own to promote. And if this were so, then every man, even every person, with his/her own interests should be able to run for office. Perhaps they should not, because they lacked the ability and willingness to deliberate and compromise. But even Hamilton, from whom we heard earlier, and unfavorably, on the nature of the people, conceded in *Federalist 71* that the people were capable of right reason and reflection. They would simply too often be led astray by "parasites and sycophants."

Why, then, did the Founders not create democratic procedures or conditions that require such reflection and that minimize the influence of parasites and sycophants? If even the first Congress was deficient in having men of fit character and was instead full of those pursuing unbridled self-interests, then why not open the system to decision-making by the people themselves? Let all people pursue their own interests.

Yet still lingering was the objection that the size of this new nation prevented any kind of directly democratic decision-making. Only representative government made sense in a nation of such expanse. Well, why not have democratic decisions made more locally, then, in communities and in neighborhoods, even in regions within states rather than the entire state itself? Surely, if the basis of governing is expressing and pursuing self-interests, then all people, extraordinary and ordinary alike, know best their own interests and can argue for those interests themselves. One person who thought so was Thomas Jefferson.

Jefferson's Vision

Jefferson offered solutions to counter the arguments that the new nation was too vast and her citizens unfit for direct democracy.

To help make citizens fit for ruling, Jefferson proposed enhanced public education. To keep government safe and the nation secure, Jefferson argued, educate the people. Jefferson thought education so important that in his State of the Union Address in December, 1806, he proposed an amendment to the Constitution to legalize federal support of education. His emphasis on the importance of education for democracy is summarized in one of his best-known quotations:

> I know of no safe repository of the ultimate powers of society but the people themselves; and if we think them not enlightened enough to exercise control with a wholesome discretion, the remedy is not to take it from them, but to inform their discretion by education.[19]

Jefferson's solution to the problem of the size of the republic was to divide the entire country into wards.[20] Each ward would comprise 100 citizens. Yes, Jefferson agreed with the obvious logic: The United States was too large for all citizens to meet in one assembly. But why have only *one* assembly? For Jefferson a government was only truly republican to the extent that each citizen had an equal voice in directing its affairs. Within each ward the citizens could take charge of their lives and their concerns. But were they competent to do so? For Jefferson, politics—taking care of roads and the poor, for example—was part of ordinary life and did not require intelligence beyond a level of common sense. Common people, claimed Jefferson, are strong judges of facts.

In Jefferson's view each ward would take care of local issues. So whereas the federal government would be entrusted with the nation's defense and foreign relations, and the state governments would concern themselves with civil rights, laws, and their enforcement, the wards would focus on local concerns. For Jefferson, then, this elementary republic of wards would provide another level of democratic power-sharing, as well as another way of providing fundamental checks and balances on the other levels of government.

The federal government at this time had little influence over the local affairs and the daily lives of the citizens. So Jefferson could imagine different levels of political participation. Since the local level was the most important level for most citizens, participation there was all that most citizens would require. The ward system was set in an era without information technologies other than broadsheets and town criers. Although each ward could elect a delegate to represent the ward in county or even state business, Jefferson saw the ward's influence extending only over local matters. That would be enough to make every citizen an acting member of the government and thereby strengthen the republic.

In a real sense Jefferson's wards were also a center of education, not just for the children of the wards, but also as a training ground for citizen participation. Here was a site to "inform the people's discretion." Informing their discretion would enable citizens to practice more self-government by increasing their experience, insights, and confidence and thereby increasing their competence.

So, what does it mean to "inform one's discretion?" It is not simply transmitting information, though that is important. It is, rather, to increase one's power to judge and decide on one's own. It is deliberation. That power is increased through greater participation, through paying attention to facts and opinions, through reflecting on what is said and on what one thinks, and through presenting and challenging perspectives. As Jefferson said, "forty years of experience in government is worth a century of book-reading."

Americans were no strangers to Jeffersonian wards. For many Americans such wards were right in their midst—New England townships—and still are today. In these town meetings, then as now, the residents made the decisions that affected and affect their daily communal lives. In fact, the 19th-century New England town meeting was one of the hallmarks of American democracy, at least as far as Alexis de Tocqueville was concerned.

Tocqueville's Self Interest Rightly Understood

Alexis de Tocqueville came from France to America in 1831 on the pretense of studying American prisons but really to better understand American democracy. The New England town meeting struck him as something completely different from the institutions of government found in Europe and especially in his native France. In the town meetings citizens gathered to rule directly. If the French wanted to know what to hope for and yet what to fear (because it signified great change) from American democracy, the best place to look, perhaps the most radical place to look, was the town meeting.

But town meetings were not all there was to American democracy. Outside of New England, no such meetings existed— at least not in the same way or to the same degree. Nor was participation as active and strong across all of New England. Other currents were moving through America that dissipated democracy.

One of those currents was a movement that Tocqueville called "individualism," a phenomenon that continues today. Understanding Tocqueville's individualism requires a little background.

European countries, Tocqueville observed, had had to overthrow or gradually remove aristocratic or hierarchical ties to feudalism and its tightly controlled social structure. Because Europeans had to overcome this and the long-entrenched attitudes and prejudices that came with them, equality was vastly more difficult to establish in Europe. In America establishing equality was, therefore, much easier because there were no such ties to begin with.

In addition, as Tocqueville emphasized, America, unlike Europe, had abundant resources, especially land, of which all, rich and poor alike, could partake. All persons were therefore free to pursue their own economic prosperity. Because of the equality of conditions in America, virtually all men were free to succeed.

What occurred, then, was that economic prosperity in America became the sign of merit. In fact, it was the only accepted form of inequality. If conditions facing every person were equal—including educational, social, and political conditions—then the most salient mark of distinction would be economic success, since everyone could attain it. Indeed, economic success became the socially acceptable mark of distinction. Thus, if wealth became a sign of merit, then poverty became a sign of weak character and moral failing. Poverty was a sign of sloth, not of misfortune or poor birth.

If that were the case, then persons would want to make their mark by focusing their time and energy on creating wealth. This turned their attention away from politics and the public realm and toward the private realm. Politics would be secondary to the private pursuit of prosperity.

With their attention fixed on prosperity and their private affairs, men ceased to look to or think about others. They thought first and perhaps *only*, Tocqueville observed, of their family and close friends. This form of isolation and attempts at self-sufficiency in pursuit of self-interests Tocqueville called "individualism." People here do isolate themselves, to be sure, from the mass of fellow citizens. But they do not isolate themselves from everyone. They have their circle of family and friends. The price is that these circles become each man's own society, as the larger society is left to look after itself.

So, while class distinctions are erased through democracy, so too are those social bonds and the cohesiveness of traditional society. A sense of community, of solidarity among persons, is built upon custom. Without that, no one is obliged to be responsive to the needs of others. As a result, that sense of community is in jeopardy as men withdraw into their private circles and leave society to fend for itself.

With men focused on private matters, wealth, and the welfare of their own small circles of family and friends, all theories and beliefs are submitted only to private judgment. Being equal to all others in matters of judgment, men do not recognize any signs of superiority in any of their fellow citizens. If one is the equal of all others, then why should he yield to others' judgment when it opposes his own?

But this situation created for Tocqueville an irony: What is the basis of each man's private judgment? Is it not public opinion? Even though men had no confidence in the greater judgment of any other *man*, what could any man say to the united opinion of *men*? If all are individually equal, and all have equal access to knowledge, then the truth must lie invariably on the side of the majority, no?

Measured against any single man, or perhaps even any group of men, each person senses his equality with the others and finds no superiority among or between himself and others. But when he compares himself "against this vast entity [the majority] he is overwhelmed by a sense of his insignificance and weakness." Equal to all, he is, with regard to status, no different from any. When all are grouped together and in agreement, who is he to stand against them? "The same equality which makes him independent of each separate citizen leaves him isolated and defenseless in the face of the majority." Perhaps the most obvious example of such pressure is when a country mounts its war machine and seeks to galvanize the public behind the need to attack an enemy.

To continue the irony: Private judgments are guided, therefore, by the majority. But this is not done through each person reflecting on what the majority thinks and says. Instead, private judgment rests on each person being supplied with ready-made opinions that relieve him of needing to form his own. Each can therefore spend his time not thinking about public need but about private prosperity.

These ready-made opinions become vital to how men understand society and the world. They need these views, or need society, at least to this extent: If persons cannot have the same level of wealth as others, then they can adopt the same opinions as a sign of equality. Men need society at least for that, and through that need, men's opinions connect them with their neighbors and fellow citizens. But it turns out that men need society for much more than that.

The value of democratic participation, as we have seen, is that it turns men from a focus on their private interests and requires them to think beyond themselves. But within individualism, as Tocqueville pointed out, men are thinking only about their private interests...until they aren't. Wait...what? Why would any man participate in public affairs when the entire point of individualistic withdrawal is to focus attention on his private circle and to leave the affairs of society-at-large to itself?

Because Tocqueville sees that men *cannot* be self-sufficient within their small circles of families and friends. They are not self-sufficient in their judgments and opinions, as we have seen, nor are they self-sufficient in generating wealth or in accomplishing, well, anything. To generate wealth and accomplish things men require their neighbors and fellow citizens. Men quickly learn that even private ambitions and personal business require the aid of others. Tocqueville describes this in an image that relates to our own situation today:

> It is difficult to force a man out of himself and get
> him to take an interest in the affairs of the whole state,
> for he has little understanding of the way in which
> the fate of the state can influence his own lot. But if
> it is a question of taking a road past his property, he
> sees at once that this small public matter has a bearing
> on his greatest private interests, and there is no need
> to point out to him the close connection between his
> private profit and the general interest.[21]

Suddenly even private matters, those seemingly about self-interests, take on a public face—like the new road past one's property. If someone is going to get things done, then he needs the cooperation and approval of others, even if those things at first blush seem solely pertinent only to oneself. Tocqueville supplies another homely example: "Men chance to have a common interest in a certain matter. It may be a trading enterprise to direct or an industrial undertaking to bring to fruition; those concerned meet and combine; little by little in this way they get used to the idea of association."[22]

Here Tocqueville describes "self-interest rightly understood." Self-interests are often and almost always tied to "public" interests; that is, tied to the interests of those other than yourself. And even when they are not, you might well need to enlist the help of others in your enterprise. But why would others help with something that does not benefit them? Because they see that they will surely need the help of others on some enterprise of their own, and if they help now, then they can count on others to help them on some other occasion.

Through these mutual endeavors persons are brought out of the isolation of individualism. They actually prosper when they join with neighbors and other fellows in civic and political participation. "When some view is represented by an association, it must take clearer and more precise shape...An association unites the energies of divergent minds and vigorously directs them toward a clearly indicated goal".[23] Over time, this frequent participation in associations exercised what Tocqueville called "local liberties"—which lead citizens to value the affection, abilities, and lives of their neighbors.

To illustrate self-interest rightly understood, consider the following example as described by Daniel Kemmis, currently a writer and formerly the mayor of Missoula, Montana, and the Speaker of the Montana House of Representatives.[24]

In the early 1950s, when Kemmis was about eight or nine years old, his family wanted to tear down their barn that had suffered greatly over the years from the winds that swept across the high plains of eastern Montana. To do so and to raise another barn, they enlisted, as was the tradition and the necessity, the help of their neighbors. But Kemmis' mother did not want her children associating with the children of neighbor Albert Volbrecht, for his children were given to obscene language and lewd stories. But the Volbrechts were neighbors and "had to be at the barn raising, just as they had to be there when we branded calves. They were neighbors, and that was that…[O]n those Montana plains, life was still harsh enough that they had no choice. Avoiding people you did not like was not an option. Everyone was needed by everyone else in one capacity or another".[25]

This story, Kemmis says, illustrates the need for people to work together to achieve the common good. In this case that "good" was pitching in to help one's neighbors raise a barn. The circumstances demanded cooperation; it was in everyone's interest to pitch in. As neighbors, they had no choice, for life was tough, and all had to help one another. Such help was necessary and expected. Otherwise, one could not count on others' help when that help was required.

As said, this is an example of Tocqueville's self-interest rightly understood. All could see, or sense, that it was in their own best interest to help a neighbor, for that neighbor would help when the positions were reversed. Notice what is involved here: Helping out a neighbor is not always only the rose. Also come the thorns. Indeed, where the interests conflict—the need to raise a new barn versus the desire to keep the Kemmis children away from the Volbrecht children—the solution is not to abandon either one, because both are in the Kemmis's interests. Why not seek an alternate way of keeping the kids separate once the families are together? Surely, there must be other ways than not inviting the Volbrechts? There were other families present; there were probably other distractions, other playmates, or older children to supervise.

By the end of the day, Kemmis's mother probably liked neither Albert Volbrecht nor his children any better. "But that day, and many others like it, taught them something important. They learned, whether they liked it or not, a certain tolerance for another slant on the world, another way of going at things that needed doing. They found in themselves an unsuspected capacity to accept one another. This acceptance, I believe, broadened them beyond the boundaries of their own likes and dislikes and made these personal idiosyncrasies seem less important."[26]

However much we may doubt that Mrs. Kemmis ever came to accept the ways of the Volbrechts, we can agree that she could see the interplay of self-interests. Deliberative democracy could have the same effect. Yet it is important to stress that what stimulated such interaction on the plains of Montana is the same kind of enlightened self-interest that stimulated Americans in Tocqueville's time and that would stimulate them today in deliberative democratic arenas.

What is not behind these interactions is some abstract or preordained notion of the common good or public interest that participants must think about or serve. A common good may develop in or come out of participants' deliberations; it may even transcend their self-interests. But that good is made in common by those who come to press and by those who come to discover their own interests. Politics on the plains of Montana or on the streets of Chicago is not about beginning with exhortations to put aside one's self-interests and think instead of the common good. Mrs. Kemmis put aside one self-interest to serve another self-interest. What brought the families together was not some grand moral scheme, nor mutual affection, nor the recognition of affective ties. It was the exigencies and hardships of life that threw them together. It was self-interest rightly understood lived out on the Montana plains.

As with so much else in Tocqueville, self-interest rightly understood rests on an irony. Citizens withdraw from the public affairs of society and retreat into those private interests that affect their sub-societies of friends and family. Yet those private interests cannot often be attained without the cooperation of others beyond each sub-society. So people come out of those small circles, emerge from their individualism, to attain the very things that drove them into isolation in the first place. Political interaction, then, is not a sacrifice for one's fellows. It is not altruism. It is, instead, the method for getting things done—things important to oneself, one's family, and one's friends.

Without this kind of political participation today, without a democratic forum in which citizens can meet to make decisions which affect them directly, people will continue to isolate themselves in their private worlds and leave society to take care of itself. In such a situation, men can tell stories about being self-made men, about going it alone, pulling themselves up by the bootstraps. But somebody made those bootstraps; there is the very strong chance that that somebody was not the man pulling them up. Somebody else made those boots, the socks on the feet that go into the boots, and the pants that go over those boots. Somebody else also built the road that self-made men are going it alone on; somebody else helped make them the persons they are. No personal narrative can fail to recount those individuals and social settings along the way that were central and even formative to their life stories. No one goes it alone; no one gets anywhere or does anything without a connection to others. We may think that we do, because we fail to look beyond the small circle of family and friends at what the community or society has made possible for that circle to thrive. Democratic institutions that provide direct deliberative decision-making on issues that affect our lives can bring people out of individualism and let them see the full social context in which they live.

When citizens are entrusted with managing their affairs, as Tocqueville noted, then they develop an interest in the public welfare. That becomes part of their self-interest; and when it is a part of their self-interest it becomes incumbent upon citizens to participate if they wish to pursue self-interest. But to be able to manage their own affairs—all the issues that affect them and move them and define their lives—then citizens have to have the democratic mechanisms for doing so when they re-enter society. Otherwise, they will just retreat back into their small circles, thinking themselves rugged individuals.

Citizens are not taught to serve; there will be no need to socialize them into participation when the democratic mechanisms exist for making rules and laws directly. Rather, it is the discipline of self-interest rightly understood, the pursuit of self-interests through political participation, that will shape their communal

53

and social bonds. The virtue of thinking in terms of the public good is a by-product of the practice of participation.

For Tocqueville, then, one undertakes the obligations of democracy because one understands and furthers his own interests by doing so. To pursue those interests requires interaction, which is promoted in Jeffersonian democracy. Thus, to enjoy the benefits of that system, one must participate in it and undertake those obligations that sustain it.

Meanwhile, our democracy, as Jefferson noted, must educate future citizens to avoid individualism by "informing their discretion"; that is, by using schools to educate the young in the skills of deliberation and by having students practice deliberative participation (see Chapter 7). An education in deliberation, built upon the skills and experiences of democratic participation, would itself be an illumination of self-interest rightly understood, which Tocqueville described as "the best suited of all philosophical theories to the wants of men in our time" and as "their strongest remaining guarantee against themselves."[27] Educate the young to have clear judgment and see the need for working together. Bring them also to understand the need for democratic mechanisms that promote the pursuit of those interests. Necessary for this education is the encouragement, if not the inculcation, of the habit of attending to what is in front of each person: That self-interests are attained through public deliberation.

What follows is an example of one way to encourage this: Turn every school into a community managed through deliberations by students, faculty, and staff. Now, we might be accustomed to teachers having some control over questions related, say, to the curriculum. And we certainly know that students learn from discussing with fellow students and their teachers in classes. But we have in mind the school community—students, teachers, administrators, and staff—deliberating together on how to maintain and change the schools. As John Dewey argued, let students make decisions about *real* problems and *real* concerns, not ones invented within their readers and math books; make the school itself part of the curriculum. Is it not, for example, in the students' self-interest to control the very environment in which they spend so much of their lives during the academic year? This could surely be one way to have students get out of themselves, out of their tender version of individualism, and come to see the value of deliberation and cooperation in addressing problems. (Once again, see chapter 7.)

Individualism, Tocqueville says, is misguided judgment, for men think that they are self-sufficient when, in fact, they must actually band together to pursue their private interests. When they come to see that these interests can best be achieved—and sometimes can only be achieved—through collective effort, then is self-interest rightly understood. Citizens might also come to realize through deliberation with others that their own immediate interests run counter to their long-term interests. Thus, such citizens could learn to accept occasional losses for the sake of those long-term interests.

Many citizens do, and will, enter the political arena with their own personal interests that they wish to pursue. They sometimes think, properly or improperly, that if others understood and then also came to hold those interests, then the community would be better off. They come to politics, therefore, both to achieve those interests and to persuade others of the benefits of those interests. In a direct democracy this could be the precise mindset of a citizen wishing to press his own interests. Initially he wants to convince his fellow citizens to see the benefits of his interests.

But deliberative procedures could also lead to dissuasion, not persuasion, as the flaws in or limitations of a person's interests are pointed out. The interests could then be modified, abandoned, transcended, or even pressed further, though, presumably, without much hope of persuasion. When an interest, private or public, wins the day, it should be an indication that behind it lies a superior argument manifesting its superior merit. Reasoned opposition by those who have objections to or problems with an interest is the best way to present the ramifications of that interest missed by those who favor it. The discussion is thereby elevated to whether that interest really is good for everyone. The case must be made in those terms if an interest has any chance of winning. Otherwise, an interest can be readily dismissed, and should be, as narrowly self-serving.

As Tocqueville observed, in serving oneself one is, or should be, also serving one's neighbors; in serving one's neighbors, one is also serving oneself. But citizens, he continued, need to *see* that connection. Because of their "individualistic" proclivities, they cannot simply be told. Deliberation enables one to see, to grasp with insight. Without the reciprocal sharing of experiences through democratic deliberation, self-interests will revert to or remain the pursuit of narrow and often exclusionary interests.

Finally, persons often need to participate in deliberative processes to *discover* what their interests are. To discover interests persons need a politics that combines deliberation, personal reflection, and action. Self-interests are not, then, just brought to politics or changed in politics. They are also discovered through and constructed in deliberations. Take immigration as an example: A group of participants, made up of students and former federal workers, Tea-Party members and undocumented workers, teachers and bankers, meet to discuss what to do about persons crossing illegally from Mexico into the United States. After a couple of hours of exchanges, some of them heated, this group begins to see that despite all of their differences and opposing views (on this issue and many others), they agree on a version of the "dream act" that none of them had thought of on their own and that no one had brought to the deliberation. They discovered this by deliberating together on the issue of immigration. We witnessed this ourselves with a group composed of such people when one of Jack's students, Jenny Reich, led an all-day deliberation on immigration at Arizona State University in October, 2010.

The aim of political deliberation, then, is not only to provide a range of perspectives on possible solutions to the problems facing the citizenry. It is also to enlighten each citizen as to his or her own wants, needs, and interests in light of competing claims. Whenever we think that we have made up our minds as to what our interests are, or what is in our interest, a diversity of contrasting points of view provides new information and requires us to compare what we think with those other positions.

Our history is not about a dream that did not materialize. It is, instead, about the beginning of a democratic journey. That journey is not steadily progressive, moving inexorably toward greater and greater democracy. The journey is uphill and down, showing twists and turns, stops and delays, pushes and demands for more democracy but also pull-backs from and concerns about democracy. But our nation might be on the brink of a direct, deliberative democracy; on the brink, that is, of 3-D Politics. One example of that is the presence already within our democracy of one form of direct democracy: initiatives. How initiatives fit within our own direct, deliberative democratic framework is the subject of the next chapter.

CHAPTER THREE

What's Wrong with Initiatives?

The states ratified the Constitution that was written by the Founders, adopting representation as the form of decision-making in the republic. The consequence of this acceptance was a total lack of participation by the general citizenry in the making of the laws. Nevertheless, beginning in the latter part of the twentieth century, there has been a slight movement toward more "direct" democracy in the form of ballot initiatives. When there are issues that legislators do not want to address, the people can propose an initiative and place it on the ballot for a popular vote. Since 1974, when Californians passed (the now infamous) Proposition 13 that rolled back property taxes, there has been an increasing number of initiatives placed on state ballots. In twenty-four of the fifty states, citizens propose initiatives when they feel their state legislators are not responsive to some pressing political issue. These citizens are engaging in a form of direct democracy.

For example, in nine states and Washington, D.C. marijuana has been legalized for recreational use. The issue of legalizing medical marijuana was something that legislators did not want to confront. Many elected representatives thought that proposing the legalization of marijuana might make them popular among some citizens but would probably ensure that they were not reelected. Instead, some citizens themselves proposed such legislation in the form of ballot initiatives. Even as the number of initiatives has increased, however, over the last few years, the consequences wrought by the initiative process have been heavily criticized.

As previously mentioned, David Broder, in his book *Democracy Derailed*, expresses grave concerns about this new form of direct democratic participation, even to the point of claiming that initiatives are "derailing" our democracy. According to Broder, citizens proposing laws (rather than relying exclusively on their elected representatives to do so) is dangerous.[28] It seems ironic that Broder would consider citizen legislation as somehow threatening "democracy;" democracy is supposed to be *rule by the people*. Do voter initiatives threaten the "republican" nature of American government? Let us consider Broder's claims.

In the final paragraph of the book, Broder summarizes his two main concerns about initiatives: 1) that the initiative process has been "co-opted" by special interest groups and 2) that the initiative process leads to "laws without government."[29] He makes this indictment with very little evidence, instead relying on some anecdotes about initiatives and his use of two important terms, "special interest groups" and "democracy." Although Broder includes some interesting stories of initiatives gone awry, he makes no effort either to define these two important terms or to be consistent in how he uses them. A more careful look at how Broder uses the terms "special interest" and "democracy" may lead one to suspect that he manipulates those terms to suit his purposes. The misuse of these terms, coupled with Broder's lack of systematic research, could lead people to conclude that initiatives pose a threat to democracy where none actually exists. Let us examine Broder's two concerns more carefully.

Concern About Special Interest Groups

When Broder claims that initiatives have been co-opted by special interest groups, he offers a serious criticism that is easily remembered and often repeated. It is not difficult to tap into Americans' fears about the power of money and special interests in our government, because there are plenty of historical examples of such abuse. One such example is the contention that it is almost impossible to pass legislation favorable to solar energy because of the influence of the oil and gas lobbyists. Broder does not clarify, however, what he means by "special interest groups," nor does he explain why any initiatives proposed by these groups must necessarily harm the public. Instead, Broder relies on the phrase "special interest groups" with no clear definition of who or what this constitutes.

The benefit of using such a catch-phrase is that there already exists a ready-made bias against and mistrust of the very notion of a "special interest group." Broder relies heavily on this presumption in his second chapter, "Power to the People." There he sets the stage against initiatives by noting the trend toward the use of huge amounts of money in campaigns to promote or oppose various initiatives related to issues such as insurance reform, environmental regulation, tax reform, and education. The reader is led to believe that all such initiatives have been co-opted by special interest groups.

In his examples Broder equates "special interest groups" with various proposers of initiatives, including "big money," "corporate interests," "crackpot millionaires," and "political entrepreneurs." So, a "special interest group" consists of any private individual on a mission such as the woman who started Mothers Against Drunk Drivers (*MADD*), or huge corporations like Shell Oil Company. Furthermore, Broder's concern about initiatives rests on his assumption that all "special interest" initiatives are sponsored by "big money," even though several of the examples that he cites were actually initiatives proposed by broad-based grassroots movements. In addition, Broder fails to provide evidence that money prevails in the outcome of initiatives; in fact, what follows is evidence to the contrary. Before examining that evidence, however, we will examine another omission of Broder's..

In his book, Broder fails to distinguish between the various types of sponsors of initiatives and all the possible beneficiaries of initiatives. Not only can sponsors of initiatives be individuals, groups of concerned citizens, corporations, multi-millionaires, and philanthropists, but the beneficiaries (or people affected by the initiative) can also be equally varied. In order to make claims about the effects of initiatives, it is important to distinguish between the sponsors and the beneficiaries. For example, a millionaire philanthropist might sponsor an initiative that actually benefits the general public; Broder never mentions such a scenario.

A brief examination of studies by initiative scholars Elisabeth Gerber and Shawn Bowler reveals the limited and complicated influence of special interests and big money in the initiative process.[30] For example, when Gerber studied the relationship between initiative spending and interest groups, she found that broad-based citizen support usually triumphed over big money. The opinions and votes of Americans are not always swayed by big money, as Broder implies.

To demonstrate this, researchers have distinguished among types of initiatives based on both the sponsors and the beneficiaries. In *Citizens as Legislators*, Todd Donovan and some of his colleagues identified four types of initiatives based on who sponsors the initiative and who will benefit from it.[31] According to this research, the initiative sponsors as well as the beneficiaries of an initiative may be characterized as either "narrow" or "broad." David Broder makes no such distinctions in his book.

A closer look at Donovan's research helps to clarify such distinctions. For example, there are "Interest Group" initiatives wherein a narrow group challenges another narrowly defined group. In California when trial attorneys battled insurance companies with competing initiatives, both the sponsors and beneficiaries were narrowly defined. This is the kind of big-money, narrow-interest initiative on which Broder rests his critique of the entire initiative process.

But Donovan and his colleagues identify three other common types of initiatives. One of those is "entrepreneurial" or "populist" initiatives in that they are proposed by a broad or diverse group of citizens against a narrow group, thereby limiting the negative consequences to a smaller group. Initiatives that propose taxing the rich or proposing a carbon tax on corporations exemplify such initiatives, which target narrow groups that bear the costs to support a broader, more diverse group of beneficiaries. This type of initiative is also called "populist" in that both the sponsors and the beneficiaries are part of a broad, diverse group.

A third type of initiative is similarly split between broad and narrow actors. Called a "Client Politics" initiative, this initiative is proposed by a narrow group wishing to affect the public more broadly. Examples of such initiatives are Philip Morris' campaign against smoking regulations and energy industry groups contesting regulations specific to their industry.

The fourth type of initiative constitutes what Donovan and his colleagues term "Majoritarian Politics," those that set broad diverse groups against one another. Criminal justice, governance, and social and/or moral issues fall into this category. For example, initiatives regarding the legalization of marijuana for medicinal purposes pitted two large segments of the population—those in favor and those opposed—against each other.

Between 1986 and 1996, there were 54 general election initiative contests in California alone, the state from which Broder draws most of his stories. Donovan and his colleagues categorized each of the 54 initiatives into one of their four different initiative types.[32] Californians voted on seven "Interest Group" (narrow group against narrow group) initiatives, seven "Client Politics" initiatives, thirteen "Entrepreneurial/Populist" ones, and twenty-seven "Majoritarian Politics" initiatives. As noted earlier, Broder contends that special-interest battles dominate the initiative contests. However, according to the Donovan study, only 14 of the 54 initiative contests were initiated by "narrow groups," while more than half of the 54 would meet Broder's definition of "public interest" initiatives; that is, those sponsored by a broad array of citizens. Indeed, what the researchers found was that there were far more examples in California of broad public groups, or entrepreneurs representing broad groups, using the initiative process to defeat narrow interests than examples of narrow interests defeating broad-based public interests.

Broder's failure to recognize any difference among initiative sponsors led him to a generalized attack on all initiatives. But the evidence demonstrates that most initiatives fall into categories too broadly supported to be considered "special-interest." Further, Broder assumes that simply because an initiative receives substantial funds from individuals ("crackpot millionaires," as he calls them) or small groups, then the initiative threatens the public. Again the evidence does not support the claim. Researchers who attended to both the sponsors and the beneficiaries of initiatives found that the public can, and often does, benefit from initiatives sponsored primarily by smaller groups or individuals. Initiatives can provide the general public the opportunity to register opinions on issues that otherwise might remain solely inside the walls of the legislatures.

In conjunction with his concern about special interests controlling the sponsorship of initiatives, Broder implies that "big money" buys initiative victories. Among his complaints is the high cost necessary in running an initiative campaign, which leads to his belief that "only the high spenders can win." However, initiative scholars such as David Magelby and Elisabeth Gerber have found that many other factors affect an initiative campaign's outcome. For example, in separate research projects both scholars have shown that money spent by opponents of an initiative has greater impact than money spent by the sponsors of the initiative. Magelby cites many cases in which the high spender lost a campaign because of the efficacy of the opposition's message.[33] Gerber's research includes examples in which the biggest spender lost, such as Philip

Morris's failed campaign to loosen stringent local anti-smoking regulations. In direct contradiction to Broder's claim, Gerber found that initiatives funded by "citizens' interests" were more likely to pass than those funded by "economic interests."

Although Broder has done some credible reporting, he has done more than report facts on initiatives. He has condemned initiatives as special-interest vehicles that threaten the public interest. However, evidence from more than one broad research study of initiatives demonstrates that most recent initiatives in California were, in fact, sponsored by or worked to benefit broadly based public groups. These initiatives may have been expensive and money may have mattered, but neither "big money" nor "special interests" are the sole factors determining whether an initiative will be successful.

"Laws Without Government"

Broder's second argument against initiatives is that the initiative process, or more direct democracy, leads to "laws without government." Broder argues that because initiatives are not proposed and debated in the state legislature, the initiative process is a radical departure from the checks and balances inherent in the legislative process. Broder cites several examples of what he calls policies made not by government but by "initiative." In 1998, for example, voters across America adopted initiatives that achieved goals as varied as ending affirmative action, raising the minimum wage, banning billboards, restricting campaign spending and contributions, expanding casino gambling, banning many forms of hunting, and allowing adopted children to obtain the names of their biological parents.[34]

Broder complains that not one of these decisions was made through the time-consuming process of passing and signing bills into laws guaranteed by, in his words, our "republican" form of government. Rather, these laws were proposed and passed by the citizens themselves. As he traces the historical development of initiatives in America, Broder makes the case that average citizens proposing and passing laws is un-American.

The initiative process, according to Broder, "had its roots in the beginning of the last century, when Populist and Progressive reformers promoted the initiative..."[35] However, there were much earlier proponents for citizens' directly participating in the making of laws. As discussed in Chapter Two, ancient Athens was an example of this, and in the 18th century Rousseau argued that a republican form of government required an "active citizenry" from whom the lawmaking function could not be alienated. Of course, the Founding Fathers disagreed, and, as Broder acknowledges, Madison's *Federalist #10* is the definitive justification for America's distinctively republican system of government; i.e., a republic in which the lawmaking function is delegated to representatives. This distinction reflects an important shift in the definition of a republic. Broder only emphasizes "representation" as the republican nature of America's present government. Until Madison's *Federalist #10*, however, "representation" was not one of the distinguishing features of a republic. A republic has other elements that are equally important. Our present republican form of government relies on a combination of the following:

1. Elected representatives
2. Separation of powers (Executive/Legislative/Judicial Branches)
3. Mixed government (President/Senate/House of Representatives)
4. A written constitution and the process by which to amend it, and
5. Judicial review

The initiative process, or laws made directly by the people, at most threatens only number 1, above, assuming it threatens anything at all. Nothing about the initiative process is a threat to numbers 2 through 5. Initiatives must be constitutional and are subject to judicial review, and no proponents of initiatives are arguing at present to disband the three branches of government as the system of checks and balances. The only revision to the traditional process for making laws is that initiatives are not "initiated" in the legislature but are brought by the people themselves. Thus, the people who might rightly be worried about this are elected legislators; they might be out of a job. However, there have not been any serious movements to disband either the U.S. Congress or state legislatures. Rather, initiatives have been used as an additional way to create legislation, not as a replacement for our present system.

Indeed, many representatives themselves endorse the initiative process because it allows them to relegate controversial issues for the voters to decide. As Broder noted, difficult issues such as euthanasia, legalization of marijuana, green space, property-valuation problems, and education bills are the types of legislation being moved from the legislatures back to the public through referenda and initiatives. One example of this was when California legislators could not get insurance companies and the auto industry together on the issue of tort reform, they eventually sent it to the voters.

Thus, the title of Broder's book—*Democracy Derailed*—seems misleading at best and mistaken at worst. The initiative process does not threaten "democracy," since democracy means "rule by the people." Nor does it threaten the "republican nature" of our democracy, since four of the five elements mentioned previously are not threatened by initiatives. At best, Broder might argue that initiatives threaten the "representative" element of our republic. But since many representatives themselves see the value of sending some issues to the public for direct legislation in the form of initiatives, it is difficult to see what the problem is. Perhaps Broder really is trying to argue that citizens should not be allowed to propose and vote directly on laws. Unfortunately, this seems a reasonable reduction of his "argument." After careful examination of the terms involved, however, it seems misguided to claim that initiatives—citizens' proposing and voting directly on laws—are either undemocratic or anti-republican.

Although special interest groups and citizens' making laws are Broder's primary concerns about initiatives, he also considers a few others. One such concern is that if direct democracy is fostered through the initiative process, then the result could be a government of simple majority rule. The concern is that straightforward majority rule can lead to the infringement of certain minorities' constitutional rights. However, direct democracy does not necessarily entail simple majority rule any more than representative democracy avoids majority rule. Minority rights can be protected by other aspects of a republican form of government, such as constitutional rights and judicial review. The initiative process, *per se*, does not entail the problem of majority rule. Any form of democracy, whether representative or direct, is equally susceptible to the tyranny of the majority. Thus, avoiding all forms of direct legislation because of concerns about the tyranny of the majority is misguided.

One other concern of Broder's is that when citizens propose and vote on initiatives, they do so in isolation, while legislators debate, deliberate, amend, and consider legislation *in toto* (Broder, p. 241). As a result, initiatives considered as separate pieces of legislation might bring about inconsistent or contradictory laws. In addition, state legislatures are responsible for some comprehensive legislation, such as approving the state budget. However, as Broder notes, anyone who has watched C-Span may not find the legislative process all that reassuring. Broder quotes Bismarck who said "[N]o one should watch either sausage or laws being made." In addition, Broder mentions the general distrust that the public feels toward their legislators:

> And who can seriously claim that legislators, busy with campaigning, fundraising, meeting with lobbyists and constituents, and traveling between their homes and the capitols where they work have more time for study and reflection on these matters than other Americans?
>
> As for their wisdom and conscience, we know what the public thinks. Overwhelmingly, polls and interviews demonstrate that most

Americans believe their elected officials look out first for themselves, then for their contributors, and put serving the public well down on their list of priorities. To tell American voters today that a politician is better motivated, more civic minded, and a better custodian of the commonweal than the voters themselves might be is an insult to their intelligence.[37]

Although Broder's response involves casting doubt on the legislative process in general, there are other possible responses. For example, the fact that initiatives are considered in isolation from other legislation is not cause for concern, but may be beneficial. Avoiding compromise and concessions that might occur among legislators allows voters to focus on a specific issue rather than having it intertwined with other legislation. As to the related worry that legislation created in this piecemeal fashion might result in conflicting laws, there are other checks and balances in the system that prevent the adoption of conflicting initiatives. For example, in the state of Arizona, the Legislative Council is a statutory committee of the Arizona State Legislature that reviews every law proposed and passed by either the legislature or citizen initiative. It seems that for every concern about initiatives, there is a reasonable response. As Broder himself admits, the proponents of initiatives are as committed to defending the process as the critics are determined to find fault.

Even though he has dutifully reported some accounts on both sides of this debate, Broder ultimately paints a bleak picture of initiatives and direct democracy. However, upon closer examination of his charges, one finds an interesting metaphor but not substantive arguments. Instead of arguments, Broder offers an investigative report about a series of *ad hoc* connections between actual initiatives and the reports of those who claim that initiatives are primarily fostered by special interests with bad intentions. However, Broder merely claims that special interests have co-opted the initiative process (without the substantive empirical evidence to support the claim) and then warns that a process that registers the whims of voters without checks and balances sidesteps the democratic ideal.

In conclusion, two of Broder's claims against initiatives are false. Various organizations sponsor initiatives; the beneficiaries of initiatives are just as varied. Big money interests are not the only ones voting and benefiting from the direct democratic process. Nor is this process free from procedural checks and balances. Broder claims that initiatives lack the "complex matrix of procedures designed to require the creation of consensus before the enactment of laws."[38] But initiatives are reviewed by state officials and are subject to judicial review.[39] Checks and balances are preserved. Broder's concerns about special interest groups and his conflation of democracy with republicanism have led him to conclusions about direct democracy that are overstated and without support.

Contrary to Broder's vision of derailment, the train of American government is on its procedural track. Initiatives are not inconsistent with many of the republican aspects of our government. Initiatives are also popular, as the rise in the number of initiatives since 1970 indicates.[40] Although Broder places his faith in representatives to protect the public interest, he overlooks the potential of initiatives. Through the initiative process, the public becomes more directly involved in the legislative process, with their opinions systematically registered, reviewed, and often rewarded. If "democracy" means "rule by the people," then initiatives do not derail democracy; instead, they help keep democracy on track.

However, one criticism of the initiative process that has been overlooked thus far is the concern that voting on initiatives may result in "mindless voting."[41] Persons can vote on initiatives without doing any research or gathering any information on the issue involved. So initiatives lack the deliberation that could take place as a bill is being discussed in the legislature. Deliberation is a key component for us in any form of direct democracy, since it prevents the mindless voting that undermines plebiscitary democracy and helps assure democratic legitimacy for decisions. Deliberation is our next topic for elaboration and discussion.

CHAPTER FOUR

Autonomy and Deliberation

Autonomy

Most people accept and even applaud the idea that countries should be self-determining. This means that most people want a country to determine without interference from other nations how they run their affairs, both domestic and international. Such self-determination is also known as "sovereignty." Sovereignty protects, or is supposed to protect, a country from outside interference by other nations that have different ways of doing things, different ways of living, and different priorities. In the ancient Greek world, this idea of independence from other nations, of sovereignty, was known as "autonomy."

Autonomy, perhaps not surprisingly, comes from combining two Greek words: *auto* meaning "self" and *nomos* meaning "custom" or "law." So autonomy literally means living by one's own laws, which we can abbreviate as self-ruling or self-governing. If autonomy is a good idea for nations, then why not for individuals? Should individuals be self-governing? Should they determine for themselves how to live and what to value? They should, and when they do so, they will act democratically; for making rules, laws, and decisions for ourselves is the essence of democracy.

The ancient Athenians, as we have seen, thought this way. That is why their political system was a direct democracy, with citizens in the Assembly voting on the very laws that would govern them. No representatives were necessary; citizens made the laws themselves. Indeed, most of the political offices for the Athenians, with the exception of generalships, were filled by lotteries involving all citizens.

This is not to suggest that ancient Athenian democracy is a system that American democracy should imitate. The idea of citizenship for the ancient Greeks was tightly controlled—no women, no slaves, and no resident aliens or resident workers were included. Our own democratic system has gone in the opposite direction, toward greater inclusion. But we want to add to that system the Athenian way of having citizens make some laws directly. Amidst all of his criticisms of democracy, Aristotle repeats in several places in the *Politics* that the people have collective wisdom, wisdom sufficient for making decisions for themselves.

Vox Populi, Vox Dei

In the *Politics* Aristotle argues that one who uses a product is often a better judge than one who makes it.[42] Thus a dinner guest is a better judge of a meal than the cook who prepared it. What does this view mean when applied to democracy? It means, if we accept Aristotle, that those who are subject to legislation are better judges of those laws than the legislators who wrote and passed those laws. For example, we can imagine a majority of legislators in Washington writing and passing a bill that declares that all citizens who earn over $170,000 (which, as it turns out, all Washington legislators do) receive a tax cut. Now, those legislators are not the best judges of that legislation if it turns

71

out that those earning over \$170,000 do not need a tax cut as much as those earning less do. So in this scenario, the best judges of the bill are not those earning more than \$170,000; nor those earning less. Instead, the best judges are all those, regardless of what they make, who can view the effects of the legislation from the perspective of what is best for the country as a whole, not just for themselves. Granted, this position assumes a great deal. It assumes that the best judges are those who can take into account both self-interest and the common good.

It seems on the surface, again following Aristotle, that if citizens make the laws, then they will not be the best judges of it, since they will only be serving themselves. But Aristotle is clear that citizens are those, or ought to be those, who rule (make laws) and are also ruled (subject to laws). Thus the best judge of a meal will be the cook who also eats it.

We do not have to believe only Aristotle here. Even Machiavelli, often thought to be the champion of extreme measures when ruling, commented that "a populace in power, if it is well ordered, will be as reliable, prudent, and loyal as an individual, or rather it will be even better than an individual, even one who is thought wise."[43] For Machiavelli the key phrase in the quotation is "well ordered." He meant that citizens must live under laws and within a structure of making and following laws. That is, citizens must live and act according to a constitution.

Later in the same chapter of the *Discourses*, Machiavelli wrote: "As far as exercising their judgment is concerned, one sees that it is rare indeed that the people hear two speeches upholding different policies, and do not, if the speeches are equally effective, choose the better policy. They are almost always able to understand those truths that are explained to them." In other words, the people know quality when they hear or see it.

The Social Nature of Autonomy

As we discussed in Chapter Two, Tocqueville warned that in America when wealth is the primary, or exclusive, mark of distinction, there is a tendency for people to retreat into the isolated world of family and friends and to leave society to its own devices. This move might seem a way of achieving autonomy, as one seeks to live without society and on one's own. It is a move toward self-sufficiency and, it would seem, governing oneself.

But that is not how individualism turns out. We know that in a modern society, as in 19th-century America, one cannot be self-sufficient, unless one is willing to live as a survivalist, living under a sod roof eating roots and berries. More important, isolation is not autonomy, because, as we saw, one cannot accomplish much—and certainly not all that one desires—without the help of others. It turns out that autonomy itself has a social nature and thus cannot be achieved without social ties. To be autonomous one cannot shut out the voices of others and the influences of community and society.

The first social aspect of autonomy should be obvious: persons are not born autonomous. They must learn to be so, and that learning requires social interaction. So we begin our lives steeped in relationships and even if we accept the idea that isolation from society is autonomy, we would also have to accept that the person has to withdraw from a particular society to isolate himself. That is, a person has to start within a society and then withdraw into isolation from it. Again, no one starts with isolation; we all start in a community.

So far, this much seems obvious. The more important social aspect of autonomy is that to be autonomous, one needs to give an account to others of how and why that decision was made. Why is there a need for an account? Because to be autonomous or self-ruled, then the rules and laws that one lives by must truly be one's own. These rules or laws cannot be ones that are simply borrowed from society or from others. They have to be those for which one can take ownership and responsibility. Ownership means thinking about those rules, reflecting on them, and examining their foundations and consequences. All of that information is necessary for a person to judge whether the rules and laws are good ones.

This kind of deliberation, personal self-reflection, is necessary but not sufficient for determining whether a decision is an autonomous one. In addition, to know whether these are good rules and one's own rules, is to listen to what others have to say about them. There might be information that has been overlooked; there might be other positions and opinions that one needs to hear and take into account before judging.

All of these considerations require deliberating with others and not just relying on oneself. There may be flaws and blind spots in one's thinking; you can overlook the obvious and be unaware of nuances. Deliberating with others, especially when they have different or even opposing viewpoints, brings these out. So the chances are good that through deliberation with others, participants will not overlook important information and nuances.

Here is an example. In rural Vermont there is a town with a river running through it. On the outskirts of town, children for generations have gone to a favorite place on the river to swim, sunbathe, and play. At this spot is a pipe that crosses the river and through which runs sewage from the town. Kids, again for generations, have played on and around that pipe, walking on it (or trying to), diving from it, and swinging on it. This constant use has led to breaks in the pipe where sewage spews into the river. Finally, the town council meets to decide what to do about these breaks and to discuss the money it will cost to repair them.

The council members debate several suggestions for protecting the pipe. The two that seem to have the most support involve hiring security guards—maybe college students—to watch the pipe during the summer months and fencing off the part of the river where the pipe is. Another suggestion, pressed by the mayor, is to electrify the pipe. A couple of council members point out that electrification might well harm some of the wildlife in the area. Only one council member mentions that it might also harm some of the town's children.

The council meeting was to be closed to the public, but residents of the town raised such a ruckus about this because the issue was important to them and their children, that the council relents and opens the meeting to the public. This turns out to be a benefit, because one of the residents, a man with no children himself and only recently a resident, suggests reinforcing the pipe itself. That way, the children could swing on it without damaging it, and the town could quit worrying about spills and repairs. Reinforcement would require a one-time expense and should not, then, give anyone any further trouble. The proposal is applauded, put into motion, and quickly passed. Without hearing from this resident, without having residents present at the meeting, there is a real possibility that the town council might have implemented a policy that was more expensive and less effective, because they had not thought of an action that met everyone's needs, even the children's.

To be truly our own, rules and laws must be deliberated, and that cannot be done only by oneself. To be thorough and certain that these rules and laws are right and good, one needs to give an account of one's thinking to others. One needs to share her thinking with others. Otherwise, she may be wrong about or incomplete in what she thinks. All of this means that autonomy requires consultation with others.

A person can hold all sorts of political beliefs without examining whether these ideas cohere or contradict. But these beliefs cannot be autonomously held without such examination. These rules to live by might be simply borrowed without thought from one's cousin or one's favorite politician. One cannot be self-ruling or self-governing without examining and reflecting on the nature, scope, and consequences of these beliefs.

We do not have to imagine scenarios to illustrate this idea. We can find such scenarios living at political rallies today. At the beginning of the health-care debate, at certain Tea-Party rallies, people displayed signs, handmade, that read "Keep Govt out of my Medicare" and "Don't Steal from Medicare to Support Socialized Medicine." If autonomy requires that we own the rules and laws that govern our lives, then the people carrying these signs have to take responsibility for owning these ideas. Responsibility means being able to give an account to others, and respond to what others say, including when they challenge our own beliefs.

A few moments of reflection and of deliberation with others would have shown the fallacy of what was evident on the signs: Medicare is a government program that provides health care to older citizens. If we actually "kept government out of Medicare," then there would be no Medicare at all. Likewise, it is in reality a "socialized" program; that means, simply, that it is run by the government. Medicare is not a private system of health care that our government would betray by "stealing" from it to begin government-supported health programs.

People had not thought through what they wrote on their signs, because they had not thought through what they were thinking about health-care programs. Most likely, they had borrowed these ideas from something they had overheard, or did not quite hear, from a close friend or relative or shock jock. They had not thought about these ideas, and thus they could not hold these ideas autonomously.

Why is this important? Perhaps those persons do not care about being autonomous. That is fine. Freedom of thought permits people to hold and to act on all sorts of half-baked and wacky ideas. But if we take seriously the idea of being self-governed, if we want to be the author and owner of the rules that define and give direction to our lives, then we want those rules and laws to be well grounded and made carefully. That requires deliberation.

What is democracy but collective self-rule? And what is democracy, then, but the collective form of autonomy or autonomous decision-making? We need to be democratic if we are really going to live autonomously. Therefore, the kind of democracy that we need will be one in which we can author many or most of our decisions, not delegate decision-making to someone else. Our kind of democracy will be deliberative, so that we can share with others our thinking and perspectives. Ours will also be one in which we can own our decisions. That kind of democracy will be direct, so that we ourselves participate directly in making the laws and rules that affect our lives. Thus to be autonomous as individuals and as a society we need direct deliberative democracy.

Deliberative Democracy

One might argue that autonomous decisions are fine for one's private life. But public life, the political life, is too complicated. We do not want average citizens, some might say, trying to make laws that govern important social and political issues—such as abortion, gun control, legalization of drugs, immigration policy, physician-assisted suicide, end-of-life care, tax rates, and the like. Yes, but we do. On what basis do we elect representatives and officeholders? On the basis of the positions that they take and their promises to act on just these issues. We vote for representatives because we think that they will do in office what we want done. But sometimes, and perhaps often, representatives do not do what they promised and what we want. Therefore, to avoid the ongoing disappointments with these "middle men," we should, instead, represent ourselves. Who knows better than we do what we think about those issues important to our lives and important to our way of life? When we recognize that our own positions are partially formed through conversations with others holding different views, then the answer to who represents us is "no one."

On the other hand, if we think that no citizen needs to hear the viewpoints of others or needs to entertain positions opposite her own, then we don't have to qualify the answer in any way. It is still "no one," but now it is "no one...ever." Does that seem reasonable? Can I never be wrong in what I think or believe? Can I always rely upon my own judgment, regardless of how quickly I have made the decision or whether I have borrowed that thinking from some group's literature that tells me what they think but not why they think it? If the answer here is equally an unqualified "yes," then we can still have direct democracy with citizens making laws. But under these circumstances many of those citizens may be content with some or little knowledge of the issues; some may have no knowledge of the issues at all. Some might simply react to what their brother-in-law said, what the 30-second ad told them, how well-dressed the spokesperson for one side was, the last thing someone said to them on the issue, or just what feeling they had when they decided to cast a vote. And that vote could be cast at home or on the road, because we might as well install automatic voting mechanisms on our computers or televisions or phones, so that citizens can vote whenever it is convenient, regardless of what the citizens know or don't know about the issue. Instantaneous democracy; effortless democracy; that can mean thoughtless democracy.

This is not the kind of democracy that we advocate, because this captures the bad aspects of democratic participation and ignores the good. Look back to Aristotle: Citizens are capable of exercising vast collective wisdom, but to do so they must deliberate together. One cannot really judge a meal by looking at the recipe; one needs to smell it and taste it. One needs to participate in it and to share thoughts and reactions with others. Nobody on *Top Chef* is ever judged by one judge alone. There is always some level of deliberation among the judges. With regard to democracy, this means that citizens need to discuss with other citizens the nature and possible consequences of social and political policies. Those discussions can be intricate, even complex, but citizens can handle that. We have the evidence of this from juries and from citizen discussions held across the country, which we will explore later. First, let us see what deliberation demands of us and why it is essential to direct democracy.

Some people believe that our representative democracy itself is already a form of self-rule. One basis for this belief is that representatives derive their authority from the consent of the governed. After all, constituents vote representatives into office. Additionally, these representatives, if voted into office, can be voted out of office. That power rests with the people, and our electoral system thus resembles people's autonomy.

Yet representative democracy does not seem to be within the spirit of what we mean by directing and authoring our own lives.

Instead, we are electing someone to do that for us, when the issues involve social and political policies. Having something done for us is not self-ruling or self-governing, even if it is done in our name.

We are reminded of Jefferson's concept of ward democracy. His system was a way to overcome the problem of the vastness of the republic and a way to educate or "inform discretion." Jefferson's ward system today would make it possible in a large democracy for citizens to meet and deliberate. It would also elevate citizens' competence to be able to judge and decide social and political policies. This is necessary if citizens today are to exercise autonomy in public; that is, if they are to be democrats and have more control over their lives through increased democratic participation. The key to gaining that control is deliberation.

We have been insisting that autonomy requires social interaction or what we might call "public talk." That talk is not just any kind of talk, but is a certain kind. Public talk involves participants sharing information, perspectives, reasons, positions, and experiences. In short, it is what we might also call "deliberation." But why does deliberation have anything to do with discussion about "public talk"? Deliberation literally means "to weigh thoroughly," especially the weighing of evidence. Nothing in that literal definition suggests that deliberation cannot be private.

But we cannot be autonomous alone, as discussed, and, more important, the issues that we are deciding on are public, political issues. We are making the rules or laws that will govern not just our own behavior but the behavior of others as well. We think that persons living under those rules and laws are the very ones who should be making them, and we want to ensure that citizens think about the nature, scope, and consequences of those decisions. That requires, in our view, talking out the different perspectives on the issues and the possible policies that citizens bring to a setting of democracy.

A lot of this deliberation will comprise citizens explaining their views, sharing their experiences, and giving reasons. But deliberation is also about telling stories. By doing so, people provide testimony about how and why they see a certain issue in a certain way. Someone might say: "Here is what I have seen in my neighborhood. Here is how your proposal hurts my family and neighbors."

Another reason for deliberation comes from the Founders themselves. The Senate was designed to be the cool and deliberative body that would serve to offset the House and the possible rash, intemperate, and unreflective sentiments that might come out of there. The idea, however, wasn't that senators were superior to all others in being cool and deliberative. Instead, deliberation—explaining, sharing, and giving reasons—is built into the structures and procedures of the Senate. Ordinary citizens themselves are capable, in the right circumstances, of cool deliberation as well, as we can see every day when citizens deliberate on juries. Indeed, it is deliberation itself that is the key to tempering heated, impetuous, and overly enthusiastic sentiments. Therefore, we need to encourage citizens to reason together about the problems that confront them as a group, community, or nation, and, in doing so, they can come up with good rules and laws—that is, good policies.

One concern about citizens' deliberating is not just that citizens aren't capable of doing it; it is that they won't do it. They won't, because they are disengaged and disaffected. They don't want to think about or participate in politics, because their interests lie elsewhere, in private concerns and mostly in making and spending money. This attitude was summarized succinctly by President George W. Bush when he advised Americans after 9/11 to "get on with your lives, hug your kids, and go to the mall." What was the underlying message? "Don't let the terrorists disrupt our daily lives of family, work, and shopping. And don't bother responding with your own thoughts and ideas; we'll take care of that for you."

But do citizens' interests really lie elsewhere? Or is it that citizens feel that they have no power and control over decisions made in their name and allegedly on their behalf? Perhaps they do not care because they are not asked to care. There is not much deliberation by citizens on political issues, because they aren't asked to deliberate about much, if anything at all. They are asked only which candidate is better. Historically, even if citizens deliberate about candidates, they do so in private or as little more than sharing opinions—and not sharing reasons or perspectives or experiences—often only gossip on a candidate's character. When have citizens ever been asked to deliberate among themselves? Deliberation on or about what? Conducted in what way?

We are not arguing to go back to a kind of Athenian assembly where all the citizens meet to make laws. That would be impractical, despite the developments in information technologies. But if we combine something like Jefferson's wards and those technological developments, then we could have a form of direct democracy in which citizens meet in small groups to hear expert testimony and to deliberate on issues important to them, with tie-ins through different technological modalities. We will have more to say about this in later chapters.

The question is not whether we should have a direct deliberative democracy. We have provided some arguments for why we think that we can and should, and we will provide more as we move along. The question now, however, is how we could have such a democracy: on regional and local issues rather than national? in a system of representative government and participatory referenda? through various methods of interactive telecommunications? Well, we envision a system that remains in many ways representative as it is right now, but that also allows citizens to make laws for themselves; a system that is face-to-face but also technologically interactive; a system that does not require citizens to participate, but encourages and permits them to do so when the issues under discussion are those important to their own lives.

In other words, if we agree that people have the capacity for deliberation, then we should not dismiss deliberative settings for all citizens because our intellectuals and pundits can envision no way to institutionalize Athenian democracy in our sizable nation-state. If citizens are capable of deliberation and if deliberation is crucial to citizens making good rules and laws, then we must explore ways to institutionalize citizen deliberation. The results will be that citizens not only gain personal benefits from deliberation, but they also generate good social and political policy. Citizens thereby can come to a deeper understanding of the issues and a deeper commitment to their positions on those issues; they expand their own, as well as the public's views and commitments; discern the true interest of the group, community, or country; develop or increase feelings of fellowship and social solidarity; overcome apathy through feelings of efficacy; and feel that they are not only guiding their own lives, but also helping to guide the collective life.

Regardless of who participates, or when, mutual respect and recognition of the importance of differences are requirements for participation in deliberative forums. When citizens participate in making a collective decision, they must take into account the differing views and proposals offered. Considering different accounts and giving their own accounts promotes mutual respect, and the mechanism for operating in this way is built into the democratic process itself. It is not a required virtue that each citizen must have in order to participate. The Founders got this right: The political system should strive to make virtue superfluous as a requirement of participation. Instead, the democratic procedure should be a device that can take and work with citizens as they are. Jefferson recognized something like this when he proposed his ward system.

What conditions should be built in? We think that they might look something like this:

1. Free inquiry requiring freedom of thought and expression when one presents his/her positions;
2. Tolerance of diverse and divergent views;
3. Openness, the seeking out and soliciting of differences and the taking up and consideration of different perspectives as if they were one's own; and
4. Reasonableness and common sense, the undogmatic use of one's rational abilities.

Citizens come with their own interests and prejudices, but participation will demand that they move, at least temporarily, beyond those interests and prejudices. They must think inclusively, not exclusively; comprehensively, not parochially; reflectively, not instinctively. They can continue to hold to group perspectives, but they must recognize that other groups different from theirs have their own perspectives that deserve to be taken into account. Taking them into account, even when the perspectives are despicable or outrageous, does not mean that these positions have to be adopted uncritically. Taking up a perspective is to treat that perspective as if it were one's own. That is, one should consider it seriously, and that means that the perspective—its assumptions, evidence, and consequences—will be critically examined. That critical examination is to treat the perspective and the person holding it with respect, because it is taken seriously. In other words, participants cannot simply assert their positions and opinions. They must be willing and able to offer reasons why their perspective is worthy and respectable. Citizens must be able to give an account of their positions in order for those positions to be considered seriously, and that expectation is mutual.

Openness to other views is not a gargantuan demand. We expect and demand such behavior in all sorts of social situations. Democratic participation is no different. Plus, citizens can learn how to act, if they do not know beforehand, during the procedures. They can easily come to understand what is required in democracy.

Façade Democracy

A final few words about deliberation. The route to the point might seem roundabout, but it is worth making.

The focus of these chapters is easy enough to state: America cannot return to a democracy that it has never had. We are not a democracy now, and we never have been. Democracy, as we understand it, is rule by the people. The people make the decisions that affect their lives. It is as simple as that. But that has never been the case.

What we have always had, from the beginning of our nation, is façade democracy. In the old days of Hollywood, films were shot on sets of buildings and entire towns that had fronts but nothing else. From the outside, walking down the street of a town in the old West, one would see shops and saloons and hotels. But behind these storefronts were only wooden beams holding up the flat facings. The buildings, all of them, were surface only, with nothing behind the appearances.

Our democracy is now, as always, nothing but a façade, a veneer. Our politicians are often from the professional class, mostly lawyers and business-types. Regardless of their occupations, such professionals too often give rhetoric a bad name. They dissemble and maneuver and manipulate in front of us, propped up from behind by position papers from think tanks, campaign managers, media consultants, focus-group experts, lobbyists turned advisers, and advisers turned lobbyists. Too often, campaign promises are flat lies.

Deliberation, on the other hand, permits citizens, average Janes and Joes, to go behind the façades of these propped-up politicians and to discover what their positions really amount to. Remove the supports from the façade and the whole front crumbles. What do candidates and politicians have to say if stripped of their crafted stump speeches and manipulative sound bites? What would a real debate among candidates look like if they could take five minutes, 15 minutes, 30 minutes to answer a question, or if they could interrogate one another?

How long are we to believe, watching the 'fat cats' of Wall Street and big banking, that hard work and playing by the rules result in prosperity? Deliberation is the simple act of tapping on the supports of bromides like that to see what is beneath or behind them. Few façades will remain standing.

We cannot simply let the people vote without deliberation, because it is too easy for the professional manipulators to flood the public airwaves with propaganda—or, as we saw in the 2016 presidential election, outright lies that drown out everything else. The gales of rhetorical gas overwhelm, even silence, those small, if numerous voices trying to be heard. We know that even the Internet, praised for its democratic range, fails to provide the counter propositions that people need to consider when facing important topics and decisions. It is not that the information isn't permitted; the Internet is nothing if not ecumenical in what is available. Instead, research shows that people tend to seek out voices like their own.[44]

Democratic deliberation as we envision it provides just such counter propositions, because they come from fellow participants' own lives and experiences. It is built of that. By deliberation we do not mean anything complicated. As we have said, it is people talking together, reasoning together, exploring evidence and examples, and trying jointly to figure out the best way to achieve or resolve something.

But are citizens really capable of deliberating? That is a vital question to answer, because if they are not, then this book is merely an exercise of imagination and wishful thinking. But we think that the evidence from deliberative groups, especially juries and citizen discussions, shows that citizens are capable, fully capable, of political deliberations that can lead to good rules and good laws. We will tackle these subjects in the next two chapters. First, we discuss the idea of "legislative juries" and show how empirical studies of jury decisions endorse jury efficacy. Then we will talk in more theoretical terms, but with real-world examples, of how powerful deliberation and dialogue, especially in small groups, can be.

CHAPTER FIVE

Legislative Juries

The increasing number of ballot initiatives in the twenty-four states which have them suggests that not all citizens want to rely solely on the representative system of lawmaking. Likewise, the advent of National Issue Forums and of other similar citizen panels demonstrates a growing trend toward public deliberation. In the previous chapter we argued for the values of both autonomy and deliberation. There is a process that could meld these two trends: Legislative Juries.[45]

Why Juries

The act of deliberating is essential to citizens' fulfilling their duties on juries. Using juries for legislating, and thus taking advantage of the requirement to deliberate, can be a way to address and overcome many of the concerns surrounding the initiative process. Such concerns include but are not limited to tyranny of the majority, apathy, the absence of deliberation, and the average citizen's unwillingness to set aside biases in order to attend to the public good. The methods employed during the jury process can help mitigate such problems.

In *Democracy in America* Tocqueville discusses the importance of juries and why serving on juries is vital to democracy in America. In the chapter entitled "What Tempers the Tyranny of the Majority," Tocqueville asserts that while juries may be more or less "democratic"—depending on the composition of the jury— the process and outcome are a practice that puts vital decisions into the hands of the ruled rather than the rulers.[46]

The very acts of deliberating and arguing to consensus that occur on juries might provide a blueprint for the future of citizens' lawmaking. Philosophers from Aristotle to John Stuart Mill have argued that citizens must be involved directly in public governance to improve themselves both mentally and morally. Serving on a jury is one critical way for citizens to be involved in government. Tocqueville argues that Americans understand virtue as "self-interest properly understood"; thus, when American citizens come together on a jury to work out a public problem, they begin to recognize that contributing to the common good furthers their own self-interest, if properly understood.

The jury itself addresses the threat of tyranny of the majority because jurors are selected at random from a broad cross section of society, including minorities. People who are not involved in politics are given an opportunity to deliberate with other citizens from varied backgrounds. In addition, serving on a jury addresses the concern about civic apathy by involving a great number of citizens every year as they are called to serve on juries. It is estimated that close to 1,500,000 American citizens will be impaneled and serve as jurors during any given year. Serving on a jury provides an opportunity for deliberation, as citizens set aside their own self-interests and argue to consensus toward a common goal. Thus the paradigm of juries—a democratic and deliberative process—helps address the concerns about citizens' direct involvement in lawmaking.

There is an obvious concern about the efficacy of juries that might preclude the use of legislative juries as a form of direct democracy. Are citizens capable of making informed judgments? A controversial example of this concern is the murder trial of the celebrity football player O. J. Simpson, who was acquitted of the murder of his wife and her friend, Ronald Goldman. This verdict cast collective doubt on the reliability of juries. The general public believed that Simpson was guilty, yet the jury voted for acquittal. Many Americans believed that in this case the jury was wrong. This case is often cited during discussions of whether juries can be trusted to make good decisions.

So, how effective are jury trials? A comprehensive study comparing judges' decisions to jury decisions was conducted by the University of Chicago Law School, with a grant by the Ford Foundation, during the late 1950s and early 1960s as part of the Chicago Jury Project. Harry Kalven, Jr. and Hans Zeisel published the results in their book, *The American Jury*.[47]

In their introduction, Kalven and Zeisel state that the purpose of their book was not to decide whether the jury, *per se*, is a good institution but to determine how well juries perform.[48] Their study compared the decisions made by juries with the decisions that would have been made by judges. Using the judges' decisions as the measure of competence, the authors considered the question, "How often do the results of the jury match what judges would decide on their own?"

Kalven and Zeisel designed their research project based on a sample of 3,576 jury trials and a survey of 555 judges. The research design was fairly simple. The trial judges were mailed questionnaires about cases over which they had presided. The judges were asked to comment on how the jury decided the cases and how the judges themselves may have agreed or disagreed with those verdicts.

The two scholars examined the results in several different ways, including by dividing the data into the categories of civil versus criminal trials and by analyzing the results by region and by state. Ultimately what the researchers found was that across all categories judges would have agreed with the jury findings about

76 percent of the time. The authors then reviewed again the 962 cases where there was disagreement. They found that 40 percent of the disagreements resulted from juror sentiment about the law or juror sentiment about the defendant; 54 percent resulted from issues of evidence; and the remaining six percent came either from facts only the judge knew or from a disparity of counsel; that is, the prosecutor or defense counsel was a more skilled attorney than the opposing counsel.

Since more than half of the 24 percent of disagreements between judges and juries related to evidence, Kalven and Zeisel concluded that the 24-percent disagreement rate would be reduced by more than half when the jury and judge agree on issues of evidence. So, setting aside disagreements about evidence, the judge-jury agreement rate is 88 percent. Given that judges, viewed as legal experts, agree with the jury's decisions more than three-fourths of the time, Kalven and Zeisel concluded that juries do a *very* good job. Their conclusions continue to be affirmed by the less comprehensive empirical studies of juries done since their work.

For our purposes, we concur that juries overall are successful in their duties. But is the method that jurors use different from the methods that legislatures use when considering legislation?

The proposal for legislative juries as an improvement to the initiative process, as a process similar to jury decision-making, differs from how the state legislatures make laws in the following ways. First, debates during state legislative sessions involve a select few elected politicians. In the state of Arizona, for example, the total number of legislators in the state congress is ninety. Thus, the number of legislators involved directly in the making of Arizona's laws is limited to that number. Because of the rate at which incumbent legislators are re-elected, the number of people who are involved in lawmaking is minimal and limited to only that small number of professional politicians. A legislative jury process considering ballot initiatives would involve a greater number of citizens in a deliberative legislative process. If even ten initiatives were placed on Arizona's ballot in a given year, and twelve citizens were called to serve on each jury (in a two-stage jury process), then at least another two hundred and forty of Arizona's citizens would be involved in the process each year. Of course, the number would be even higher if numerous juries were held around the state to deliberate on each initiative. That could entail another 4,800 citizens each year becoming directly involved in creating laws.

Second, in addition to involving greater numbers of citizens in creating legislation, the legislative jury process would provide educational benefits to those citizens. Involvement in discussions concerning the public good helps to educate citizens and to overcome apathy. This direct involvement in the legislative process would also have the benefit of putting average citizens into the role of legislators. Such "hands on" involvement would give citizens a better understanding of how difficult it is to create effective legislation. This, in turn, could lead citizens to be more sympathetic toward their legislators.

The Model

We have argued for the importance of democratic deliberation and provided some justification for the benefits of jury deliberation in particular. Now we turn to describing our model of legislative juries to see how such deliberation might work in the ballot-initiative process.

Given that a legislative jury's purpose would be to create initiatives as opposed to deciding guilt or innocence, the jury trial process is not perfectly analogous. The similarities between a jury trial and our proposed legislative jury, however, include the following:

- the random selection process of 12 members;
- *voir dire* in order to uncover biases that might hinder an impartial deliberation;
- the gathering of information regarding the legislation to be done in open court, with the public invited to observe but not participate unless called upon as witnesses;

- the calling of expert witnesses to provide evidence and instructions (including attorneys who may be randomly selected to instruct the jury on matters of law, when necessary);
- and deliberating and arguing toward consensus behind closed doors.

The obvious dissimilarities between trial and legislative juries include but are not limited to the following:

- the absence of an adversarial process;
- no plaintiffs or defendants, and thus no attorneys advocating for each side;
- the presence of a neutral moderator on hand to guide the process of deliberation;
- and no verdict of guilt or innocence, but, instead, the creation of a ballot.

Because of the obvious dissimilarities, we have adopted (in part) the format for deliberation used by the National Issues Forums, one of the many forums for public deliberation that have arisen in the last decade.

National Issues Forums (NIF) have been convened around the country to promote public deliberation on important social and political issues. The Kettering Institute has created a network of Public Policy Institutes in several regions across the nation to conduct discussions among citizens on issues important to their lives. Through these Public Policy Institutes, communities are encouraged to confront critical issues in a "non-confrontational, non-partisan manner." These National Issues Forums provide large numbers of citizens with a way to develop and to express deliberative skills, while tackling real-life issues.

Trained moderators lead the proceedings in every forum organized and run by the NIF. The moderator provides an overview of the Forum's process, describes the issue, remains neutral, encourages discussion, and keeps track of the time. In addition to the moderator, every NIF meeting designates a citizen to record the proceedings. The recorder's role is to capture the proceedings by keeping a written record of the highlights of the discussion and of the main ideas proposed during the deliberation.

In order to facilitate positive and respectful deliberation, the NIF has adopted a set of "ground rules" for the forums. We proposed in Chapter 4 some minimal conditions for productive citizen deliberation. Those conditions were informed by the NIF "ground rules":

1. The moderator will remain neutral.
2. Everyone is encouraged to participate.
3. No one or two individuals dominate the conversation.
4. Listen to each other.
5. Practice mutual respect and attentiveness; really try to understand the other person's point of view.
6. Maintain an open mind. Be prepared to explore new ideas and to change the way you view the issue.
7. Everyone understands this is not a debate.
8. Speak your mind freely, but don't engage in personal attacks.
9. Address your remarks to the group. Don't hesitate to question other participants to learn more about their ideas.
10. As the discussion proceeds, try to identify the areas of agreement and disagreement. Is there common ground that could be the basis for group action?[49]

Issues forums are divided into two tiers: the "framing" tier and the "naming" tier. The work done during the framing tier helps participants to organize and structure possible policy or position options. This framing helps to bring focus to the deliberations. With a legislative jury there will be a framing jury to generate and propose possible options for the wording of the ballot issue. The second tier of public forums, or the "naming" tier, involves participants' deliberating and choosing the best alternative from the three or four possible policy or position approaches. Our legislative juries will also have a "naming" jury.

We also adopt from the National Issues Forums the necessity of beginning each deliberation session with ground rules. In the same way that traditional juries receive initial instructions from the judge, so will participants in legislative juries receive ground rules that set a respectful and professional tone for the deliberation. The instructions are clear and focus around the central idea: This is a deliberation, not a debate (which implies winners and losers). The presence of a trained moderator helps the group to stay on task and follow the ground rules.

Another important element that we adopt from the NIF is setting compromise as the goal rather than "winning." This helps the jury develop a cooperative mindset as opposed to fostering divisiveness.

Finally, it should be mentioned that even though we offer a fair amount of detail, there will be many logistical and theoretical questions that remain unanswered. Our goal is to provide as complete a vision as possible with the understanding that we may not have anticipated all the practical and/or theoretical problems.

With all this in mind, and given that most readers are already familiar with the rudimentary aspects of the jury trial process, we are ready to describe how a legislative jury might function by providing a hypothetical example.

The Hypothetical Example

An issue is referred to a legislative jury as a step in the already defined process for putting an initiative on the ballot. Of the states that allow citizen-sponsored ballot initiatives, several states have adopted regulations that limit the scope and content of any proposed initiative. These regulations may restrict the initiative to only one topic or prohibit proposing initiatives that lack funding mandates. So, this issue will have already met certain state's requirements before being referred to a legislative jury.

As said, a legislative jury borrows aspects both from the NIF and from traditional trial juries. How might a legislative jury actually function? To explain that we use a hypothetical situation.

In this example citizens in the hypothetical state of WE (the abbreviation for the imaginary state of "Weed") wish to legalize the use of medical marijuana. Legalizing marijuana for medicinal purposes has been on several state ballots recently and has been approved in a few of those states, though the legislation has not yet been enacted into law in all of those states. One reason for this might be that the federal government contends that legalizing marijuana for medicinal purposes is inconsistent with federal prohibition on drug use. Although some states have overcome this federal pressure, others have not been successful and continue to litigate the issue in the courts.

So, within our hypothetical example, the state of WE has gathered more than the required 20,000 voter signatures required to place the medical-marijuana initiative on the upcoming ballot. At this stage a framing jury of the legislative jury convenes to craft the language of several policy options, one of which will be selected by the naming jury and will appear on the ballot.

As in the current jury model, citizen participants for the legislative jury are randomly selected from some designated citizen lists (for example, census rolls) to serve. Again, as in the current jury model, the prospective legislative jurors arrive at the courthouse on the appointed day. Of course, not all citizens will be able to respond to a jury summons. For example, ill health and extreme hardship are recognized as grounds for an exemption from the duty to serve. But assuming that one has no legitimate excuse, prospective jurors show up and await selection for a specific jury. Citizens are arranged in groups of thirty to move forward to a possible assignment; the goal is to choose at least twelve impartial jurors from the randomly selected group of thirty. Those selected will receive a daily wage (perhaps something like $15.00 per hour).

As in the *voir dire* process in civil or criminal jury trials, potential legislative jurors must undergo some questioning to determine whether they have any vested interest in this legislation. For example, if someone is suffering from a disease and her suffering could be alleviated by the use of marijuana, she is excused because she has a vested interest in the outcome. Why is impartiality a requirement for selection as a juror? As noted earlier, we want jurors to deliberate their self-interests *rightly understood;* so, we do not expect participants on a legislative jury to check their biases at the door. However, it is important that the potential jurors are capable of reasonably discussing their self-interested views with other self-interested individuals. It would undermine the process for a juror to be so biased as to be unable or unwilling to deliberate. So, the purpose of the *voir dire* for a legislative jury is to ensure the selection of jurors capable of engaging in a good faith effort to deliberate on the issue. It is understandable and not detrimental to the process for people to bring their sympathies and prejudices to the deliberation, for the hope of deliberation is to bring alternative views and dispositions to the conversation. However, if someone has a substantial interest in the outcome such that he or she cannot deliberate in good faith, that person will be excused during the *voir dire.*

In jury trials the attorneys and the judge perform the questioning during *voir dire.* However, since no judges preside over a legislative jury, and no lawyers act as advocates during the process, the questioning during jury selection is to be performed by professionals trained for this function.

The individuals performing the *voir dire* (we propose that they be called *quaesitors,* the Latin word for "investigator") will be selected based on their previous training and ability to ask pertinent questions and to remain neutral throughout the process of impaneling the jury. For example, someone with a legal background or a background in psychology might be well suited for this task. Ideally, the position of *quaesitor* would be a professional bureaucratic position, similar to the position of bailiff or court reporter, so that this individual is continually on staff and randomly assigned to a jury. Random assignment of *quaesitors* to juries would help lessen the chances that the person in charge of conducting the *voir dire* might have requested questioning a particular jury in order to "stack" the jury. Another concern is that a prospective juror could have an ulterior motive and could lie during questioning in order to remain on the jury. However, at least one other safeguard is built into the process to prevent against the possibility of corrupting the jury and subverting the process.

In order to lessen the chances of corruption, the legislative jury process will involve a two-tiered approach, similar to the two types of forums adopted from the National Issues Forums. By using the "framing" jury and the "naming" jury as two separate juries with two different tasks, it is unlikely that *quaesitors* or outside forces could influence or corrupt *both* juries.

The first phase of the process consists of impaneling a jury in order to frame the issue and to propose some possible approaches to legislation. This framing jury (similar to the framing tier in National Issues Forums) is crucial to the success of legislative juries because this is the stage of the process in which a diversity of approaches will be included for deliberation and discussion. Again, following the NIF model, the purpose of this "framing" jury is to propose at least three or four different approaches to the issue. The approaches should vary greatly, even to the point of being diametrically opposed to one another, in order to assure a broad range of possibilities for discussion and deliberation by the "naming" jury.

In the second phase, after the framing jury is excused, the naming jury is impaneled to select which of the three or four approaches should be fashioned into an initiative to be placed on the ballot. The jury must select one approach *tout court* (about which, more below).

Thus, the first task of the framing jury is to read and discuss *amicus* briefs—a document filed with the court by someone who is not a party to the case—that have been solicited in accordance with a predetermined standard. These briefs will allow interested parties (who are not necessarily recognized experts) to supply information to the jury for consideration. The rationale behind such briefs is to provide a way for interested parties to inform the jury without giving oral testimony. In addition to interested parties, experts will be invited to "testify" by sharing their expertise in writing, which should ensure that only interested parties file briefs with the court.

The jury then decides how to cover information from the briefs; that is, whether the briefs are divided amongst jurors and summarized, or whether each juror reads every brief. The reading and discussion of these briefs are to be conducted in private. After discussion, deliberations on the available approaches begins.

The initial deliberations are held privately among the jury; however, as the deliberations proceed, the jurors may find that they would like to hear advice in the form of testimony from either trained experts or authors of some of the briefs. For example, the jurors could ask for a psychologist or a psychiatrist to be brought in to testify as to the addictive quality of marijuana. They may also want to hear more detail from a writer of one of the *amicus* briefs. Perhaps a group of social scientists submits a brief about the effects of legalization of marijuana in Amsterdam, and the jury may like to hear more of the details of that study. The jurors may invite experts and witnesses to testify as needed, and this testimony should take place in a public setting. As in the present courts of law, only those persons invited may testify at these public hearings.

After hearing the testimony and being satisfied that they have adequate information, the framing jury retires from the public deliberation and, in private forms, the three or four approaches. The framing jury must come to a consensus on the possible approaches; if not, then the jury must report that they are "hung." If the moderator agrees, the jury will be dismissed. If the available statistics on hung juries in criminal and civil trials may be used as a reliable guide, this should occur only rarely; that is, about one percent of the time.[50] If the jury is unable to agree on possible approaches, the state may decide that the issue be sent back to the public for the required number of signatures before it may be brought forward again. Alternatively, the state of WE may waive the signature requirement and allow for another framing jury to be impaneled immediately.

To continue with our hypothetical example involving marijuana, the framing jury settles on the following approaches to send forward to the next stage—the naming jury:

1. No legislation—marijuana remains illegal.
2. Legalize as a prescribed drug to be used only for terminally ill patients and with heavy taxation to offset some of the costs of enforcement.
3. Legalize as a prescribed drug to be dispensed at the discretion of the attending physician.
4. Legalize in small quantities (for personal use only, not for distribution and sale) for all adults over the age of 21, but with heavy taxation in order to offset the costs of education and possible addiction.

After these approaches have been formulated the framing jury is excused, and the process moves on to the work of the naming jury. The naming jury will deliberate on the three or four approaches. The goal of their deliberation is to come to a consensus on which approach will then be fashioned into a proposed ballot initiative. This jury's purpose is to select or "name" one of the approaches to become the actual initiative to be placed on the ballot.

It is important that the naming jury select their legislation from the alternatives that were formulated by the first jury. If the naming jury decides that it would like a different approach altogether or a "hybrid" of the framed alternatives, then the outcome of their deliberation would be to reframe the approaches and send them on to a new naming jury where the selection process would begin again. So, in effect, that naming jury would become a new "framing" jury, and their approaches will be sent to a different "naming" jury. This is important because if the second jury can deviate from the approaches and in essence can do whatever it wants, then the two-stage process is subverted, leaving, in effect, a renegade jury that has co-opted and possibly corrupted the process. Thus, every naming jury must choose from the alternatives already vetted by a framing jury. Of course, there can be multiple framing juries deliberating simultaneously on the same topic to come up with the three or four alternatives. Indeed, doing so necessarily involves more citizen participants from around the state.

In our hypothetical example, imagine that the naming jury has decided on the fourth approach: "legalize in small quantities (for personal use only, not for distribution and sale) for all adults over the age of 21, but with heavy taxation in order to offset the costs of education and possible addiction." The jury is now faced with formulating the legislation for the ballot. During this stage the jury may call in experts, as needed, to help them create that legislation. Before actual placement on the ballot, the proposed legislation would be submitted for review by court-appointed WE state judges who would check the proposed legislation against current statutes and relevant case law. If the jury unwittingly creates legislation that is either unconstitutional or in direct conflict with other legislation, then it will not be placed on the ballot. Of course, this should not occur because the legislative juries will hear expert testimony and have access to appropriate legal advice during both phases of the process. A list of attorneys who are experts in their respective areas could be maintained and called upon when advice for legislative juries is needed. Attorneys could volunteer their time to testify as legal experts if they wish.

If the jurors on the naming jury have agreed on approach four, then with the guidance of legal experts, the naming jury might formulate an initiative such as this:

> Adults over the age of 21 may possess up to one ounce of marijuana, or six marijuana plants, for personal use. Marijuana will be taxed, as appropriate, in order to finance educational programs on the effects of marijuana.

The initiative would then be placed on the upcoming ballot according to the applicable WE state rules and regulations governing the placement of initiatives.

Alternatively, the legislative jury might propose that no legislation be enacted. For example, some of the expert testimony may have convinced the jurors that any legislation making the use of marijuana legal really *is* in conflict with federal law. In that case the jury might decide that no legislation be proposed, because as long as the legislation conflicts with federal law it will not be enacted and would thereby be a waste of taxpayer time and money. The jury would then be dismissed and the issue set aside until such time as another group of citizens gather the requisite signatures to address the issue again at a later date. Having briefly outlined the overall legislative jury process, there are a few more details about the nature of the deliberations and outcomes.

Since reaching consensus is the goal during deliberations in the legislative jury process, a juror may be excused for a "failure to deliberate." In the applicable case law, there is precedence for removing jurors who fail to perform their duty to deliberate during a jury trial. On a legislative jury the moderator could—in accordance with the applicable state or federal statutes and accepted case law regarding a juror's removal from a jury—excuse a juror for a failure to deliberate.

On both the framing jury and the naming jury the jurors must reach consensus, so either jury could end up "hung."; the jurors on the naming jury might not formulate a proposed initiative. The hung jury in either case would then be discharged and another jury impaneled at a later date if there is impetus to continue toward legislation on that issue. If the framing jury has "hung," then the process would have to start over with the issue brought forth once again by an appropriate number of signatures from concerned citizens. However, if the state of WE deems the issue to be of pressing public concern, then the state may waive the collection of signatures and go straight to impaneling a new framing jury. As discussed earlier, if the naming jury has "hung," then the issue might be sent back to another framing jury or the process may have to start over with a new collection of signatures.

At this point, one might wonder why the juries must argue to consensus as opposed to accepting a majority or supermajority vote. After all, when requiring consensus rather than a majority, then one person can act as a hold-out and thus control the outcome. Given that one person on the jury could have that much potential power, the equivalent of veto power, this would seem to make the process both anti-democratic and anti-egalitarian.

First, reaching consensus is not the same as unanimity. In one academic department, for example, with which we are familiar, faculty often argue to a consensus on a course of action without ever taking a vote or reaching "unanimity." Rather than calling for a vote at any given time, the faculty keep discussing until everyone's views have been heard and the group has reached resolution. The faculty reaches a consensus in that everyone agrees that all viewpoints and possible courses of action have been heard and considered. The consensus is the agreement to move forward without taking a vote. Some faculty might still be dissatisfied, and had they voted, they would have voted "no." Now, however, they recognize that they have exhausted their ability to make their case and so agree to move forward. Reaching unanimity means all voting "yes" before taking action or movement. Since most jury practices involve voting and unanimity, we are proposing something else for legislative juries.

Currently, on most civil and criminal juries, the foreman must continue to poll the jurors until a unanimous decision is reached. Most jury trials require unanimity based on tradition, but according to the prevailing literature on juries, there is some evidence that requiring unanimity results in slightly better decisions than requiring only a majority or supermajority during a vote. However, even if there were no empirical data to support unanimity over majority decisions, reaching a consensus during their deliberations is an important part of the legislative jury process.

A goal of the legislative jury process is to have a group of average citizens deliberate and reach consensus about legislation on a difficult issue. You may recall from Chapter Three that Broder criticized the initiative process because it lacked the "complex matrix of procedures designed to require the creation of consensus before the enactment of laws." So, reaching consensus addresses one of the primary criticisms of the initiative process.

Another purpose of the legislative jury is to have a representative portion of the population reach a decision aimed to serve the public good, so if one or more persons cannot agree on the proposed legislation, it is possible that the hold-out(s) might represent some portion of the population that would not agree to that legislation. Thus a "hung jury" in this case would be wholly appropriate. Because the purpose of the legislative jury differs from the purpose of a criminal or civil jury, the notion of a hold-out in a legislative jury is not as problematic as it might seem and actually better serves the ultimate goals of these deliberations.

Possible Concerns About Legislative Juries

There are other concerns about possible corruption of the legislative-jury process that we need to address. We have already addressed the concern that a juror might have a vested interest and thus manipulate the outcome. This should be handled during *voir dire* and the two-stage jury process. A juror selected for one stage of the process cannot serve on the second jury. So, even though one forceful person might be able to direct one jury, she would not have any opportunity to sway the second jury.

Although this proposal for legislative juries might seem a bit radical since we argue for the use of ordinary citizens to create legislation, we are not alone. John Gastil, a professor at Pennsylvania State University, has argued for "citizen panels." These panels bring citizens together to deliberate on candidates. In *By Popular Demand: Revitalizing Representative Democracy through Deliberative Elections* Gastil recounts the story of a bond issue in the Orono school district, west of Minneapolis, Minnesota. A bond issue placed on the ballot in 1995 and 1997 failed both times. As a result, in April, 1998, the Jefferson Center, an organization dedicated to using informed, citizen-led solutions on public-policy issues, impaneled a "citizen jury" to deliberate on the needs of the school district. The twenty-four jurors listened to expert testimony and then deliberated for five days. The jury's recommendations led the Orono Board of Education to draft a third bond issue referendum that did pass.

Another example of bringing concerned citizens together to influence legislators is the National Issues Forums' "pre-legislative sessions," which have been held in at least one district in Florida. In these sessions state legislators are invited to watch the public deliberate on "hot topics" facing the legislators *before* the legislative session begins. At the first pre-legislative forum held in Florida, even though all of the state legislators from that district had been invited to attend, only one legislator did attend. This fact was published in the local newspaper as part of an article covering that pre-legislative session. The next year, again, the newspaper published the names of those legislators who attended the pre-legislative session, along with the names of those who did *not* attend. By the third year, all of the legislators from the district attended the pre-legislative session.

Another effort aimed at improving the initiative process is the Citizens' Initiative Review in the state of Oregon. The Oregon Citizens' Initiative Review is a process that allows citizens in Oregon to review and deliberate on statewide initiatives after they are placed on the ballot. The first Citizen Initiative Review was created in 2008 as a pilot project run by Healthy Democracy Oregon, a non-profit, non-partisan organization dedicated to providing evaluations of ballot measures in the state of Oregon. By May, 2011, the Oregon State Legislature had enacted a law making the Citizens' Initiative Review a part of the initiative process for every initiative placed on the ballot. A new randomly selected panel of 24 citizens is created for every initiative review in the state of Oregon. The panels are created and the process is administered by Healthy Democracy Oregon.[51]

These few examples demonstrate a movement toward more deliberative, inclusive, participatory, and direct democracy. The

103

use of legislative juries could provide a decisive next step in that direction. Since the proposal for legislative juries relies heavily on the efficacy of juries as a deliberative, democratic institution, we summarize with a quotation from Jeffrey Abramson's influential book, *We, The Jury*, in which he defends the importance of the jury system:

> I will argue for an alternative view of the jury, a vision that defends the jury as a deliberative rather than a representative body. Deliberation is a lost virtue in modern democracies; only the jury still regularly calls upon ordinary citizens to engage each other in a face-to-face process of debate. No group can win that debate simply by outvoting others; under the traditional requirement of unanimity, power flows to arguments that persuade across group lines and speak to a justice common to persons drawn from different walks of life. By history and design, the jury is centrally about getting persons to bracket or transcend starting loyalties.[52]

CHAPTER SIX

The Power of Dialogue and Deliberation

H aving established a framework for legislative juries, we need to demonstrate that citizens, your average Janes and Joes, can democratically deliberate to create good rules and laws. An example of citizens doing that can be found in the budgeting process in Porto Alegre, Brazil. Porto Alegre was the first city in the world to use participatory budgeting and thus has a history that U. S. cities—New York City and Chicago excepted—currently lack.[53]

Located in the southernmost Brazilian state of Rio Grande do Sul, at the confluence of five rivers, Porto Alegre is an important industrial and commercial port with a population of nearly one and a half million people. As with any large city, Porto Alegre has suffered from large economic inequalities. In 1989 the Workers' Party (the *Partido dos Trabalhadores* or PT), running on a platform of social justice, won the mayoral election. Once in power, their first goal was to tackle those economic inequalities, so the party instituted a participatory budgeting process. The PT removed the previous system of having the city council decide the municipal budget and replaced it with a participatory system using both representatives and direct participation by the people.

Now, every January, even with the PT out of office, "people's assemblies" are held in the city's sixteen districts to discuss the forthcoming budget, usually around 200 million dollars per year, including such issues as waste disposal, education, housing, health care, and public transportation. The people discuss among themselves their district's needs, arrive through this discussion at spending priorities, and then elect delegates to represent those priorities at district councils. Every week or two each delegate returns to his or her assembly to deliberate with their citizens about the latest ideas and plans. The delegates do not change the priorities of the people's assemblies or make decisions independent of the assemblies they represent. The Municipal Council, elected from among the delegates and representing every district, then reconciles the priorities and needs of each district, arrived at through deliberations among the people within each district, with the resources available.

The results of this participatory budgeting have been impressive in at least two ways. First, the number of participants continues to rise from its initial modest 1989 turnout. In 2003 fifty thousand residents took part in the budgeting process. No one who wanted to participate was prevented from doing so or had to pass any kind of test.

Second, as the World Bank attests, this method of budgeting has led to demonstrable improvements in city living. In 1989, when the participatory process began, 77 percent of the households in Porto Alegre had running water. Now 99 percent of households have treated water and 85 percent have piped sewage. In the 12 years between 1989 and 2001 the number of public schools in the city rose from 29 to 86. Literacy in Porto Alegre is now 98 percent.

Because no one is discouraged from participating, the poor and less well-educated have no trouble attending assemblies and speaking up, despite Brazil's reputation for racial discrimination. Perhaps as a direct result of this, the bulk of new street-paving projects goes each year to the poorer, outlying districts.

The participatory system in Porto Alegre might not fit exactly with how we might envision democratic deliberation, but it is surely an example of the people, working in concert with city officials and elected delegates, participating in a democratic decision-making process for realizing what the people themselves want and need. And the people of the Porto Alegre assemblies are not trained in the budgeting process; they do not have degrees in or experience with statistics, data analysis, or urban planning. They are simply people who have experiences living within the city and with neighbors, experiences that lead them to see what needs to be done in their districts and neighborhoods. Rich and poor, educated and uneducated, literate and illiterate, they all come together to deliberate on what needs to be done, and apparently they deliberate quite well.

How can such a process be successful with people who are set in their ways and beliefs, who won't budge from their positions no matter what they hear or what is presented to them? Such people might tolerate views that differ from their own, but that will not prevent them from digging in their heels when the time to vote or decide comes around. These people can simply outlast the longest meeting by sitting patiently, waiting for voting or decision-making time. They can appear to entertain all the different views to which they are exposed, but in reality they are just waiting to mark the ballot or push the button. Because, regardless of the arguments or evidence, such people think that their view is the right view.

All of us probably know at least one person like this or suspect that someone we know is like this. We all certainly fear that most of the electorate is more narrow in its views than what we ourselves hope or aspire to be—tolerant, wise, benevolent, open, and reasonable. How can such people participate constructively in deliberative democracy?

The presence of such people, however, is rare. At least that has been the experience of scores of people who have actually been involved over the years with citizen groups meeting to deliberate on important social and political issues. One of them, David Mathews, the president and CEO of the Kettering Foundation, has spent the past 20 years and more overseeing the National Issues Forums. His experience overseeing hundreds of such forums is that regular citizens, with strong and differing political orientations and positions, are not only willing to deliberate, but are also capable of discussing and thoughtfully deliberating on such public issues as gun control, American foreign policy, physician-assisted suicide, the legalization of marijuana, and nuclear proliferation.

On one issue dealing with energy sources and policy Mathews found that average citizens could even engage deeply with subjects that were full of scientific and technical considerations. Such considerations did not overwhelm participants, none of whom had scientific or technical expertise. When presented with adequate information, the participants had little trouble weighing the pros and cons of renewable energy sources, including nuclear energy.[54] To "weigh the pros and cons" is, as we know, another way of saying "deliberate."

Mathews's experience is not an isolated one. A study done by Holton and LaFollette found something similar:[55] A random sample of the general public, a group of 70 participants divided into six groups, was asked to deliberate on research projects involving complex technical issues and large collections of data. These groups came to the same decisions and the same judgments as the scientists with expertise in the complex science and technology involved in the projects.

So how do we square these researchers' views of ordinary citizens with a common view that most of the American electorate is apathetic, ill-informed, and narrow-minded? Such a view is reinforced by looking at the turnout for elections, for school-board meetings, or for city and town-council meetings.

But are the people who attend such meetings ever asked to do anything once there? They might be allowed to make a comment or ask the officials a question, but that is all. What, then, does "participation" at such meetings amount to—simply speechifying for a few minutes? Looking at the nature of public meetings of almost any sort, or at our elections, how much influence—to say nothing of control—over their own public lives do citizens have? Is their experience similar to that of the citizens of Porto Alegre? Outside of New England town meetings, the sad answer is almost always, "no."

People want to have an impact on issues that they care about. If we want them to have an impact, or to be able to have an impact, then we have to create new arenas for their participation. That is what participatory budgeting is about; that is what legislative juries are about. To have an impact citizens must be at the center of the process.

So, should apathetic, even grossly uninformed, people have participatory opportunities to deliberate on and decide important public issues? If we dropped these people into the middle of a group and said, "Decide what to do about the issue of school vouchers," then we might well get the very kinds of outcomes that we fear—segments of attendees sitting in utter silence; screaming participants shouting down views they oppose; contributions that are little but lists of complaints; and the group making quick and thoughtless decisions, thereby resulting in weak or dangerous policy.

In a direct, deliberative democracy NO ONE is excluded. No one today is excluded from jury duty; no citizen takes a test to see whether she or he can follow legal instructions and deliberate. That is because the system provides rules and a structure to follow. Legislative juries and deliberative democracy have rules and structure as well. We assume that people can and will follow them, and the evidence is that they can and do.

For example, consider this experience from Pete Hamill, at the time a writer for the *New York Daily News*. The paper sent Hamill to the Javits center in New York City on July 20th, 2002, to report on a deliberation held there by 5,000 residents of the city. Hamill's assumption going in was what many of us might think:

> We came to the vast hangar at the Javits Center expecting the worst. Put 5,000 New Yorkers in a room, charge them with planning a hunk of the New York future, and the result would be a lunatic asylum. We would erupt in waves of mega-kvetch. Shouts, curses, tantrums, hurled objects, nets hurled to make mass arrests. All laced together with self-righteous sound and obsessive fury.[56]

But that's not what happened. Instead, the residents were put into a precise deliberative situation, where the rules were evident and the deliberating groups were small. Hamill states:

> We [were] broken down into groups of 10, seated at tables equipped with a computer... We came... expecting the worst. Instead... [we] debated in a sober, thoughtful, civil way... All around the vast room, you heard citizens saying politely to others, 'What do you think?' And then listening - actually listening - to the replies. In this room, 'I' had given way to 'we.' Yes, the assembly was boring to look at, too serious, too grave, too well-mannered for standard TV presentation. And it was absolutely thrilling.[57]

Educators often find, as we have, that students rise to meet the expectations established for them. There are, of course, students who cannot or will not do so. It seems that the Founders of the United States had similar expectations of our citizenry.

The Founders are thought of as brilliant men who established a government on the basis of high principles. But the Founders knew, because they had experience living in the colonies, that the people living under the Constitution were not all persons of high principles. The genius of the system was that they didn't have to be. Citizens did not have to be brilliant thinkers in order to be guided by the universal moral principles that served as the foundation for the Constitution. They simply had to behave in public as if they were.

So, a Pennsylvania farmer might not care for his neighbor's opinions and way of life. The farmer might object to his neighbor's strange dress and peculiar religious ideas and might want to see public expression of those ideas curtailed. But that Pennsylvania farmer had to honor the right of that neighbor to say whatever he wanted whenever he wanted and to dress and worship however he wanted. Therefore, the genius of the Constitution is that high-minded principles such as tolerance and freedom of expression are structured into the document to require that the people follow those principles, even if people do not or cannot accept those principles as their own. Citizens in the public square must behave as if they do accept those principles; that is the key: *behaving as if they do.* The social and political situation, the context created by the Constitution, demands that they do so.

The Power of Circumstance

Participants must adapt their behavior to the rules of the procedures, whether the procedure involved is voting in an election, participating on a legislative jury, or working with fellow members of a club to set the rules for their organization. There is abundant evidence now in social psychology showing that people's behavior is to a large extent heavily influenced by the characteristics of the situation in which they find themselves. What a person brings to the situation is relevant, but the circumstances of the situation can often overwhelm the disposition of the person. The circumstances themselves can be transformational. Depending on what those circumstances are, they can transform behavior in benign directions or in evil directions. So in very difficult and trying circumstances good people can commit evil acts.

Of course, personality and situation interact. Everyone acts within situations or contexts that create their own directional pushes and pulls, and so an individual's character brought to the situation is no guarantee that he or she will act in a certain or predictable way once in that situation. At the same time, we are not

111

slaves to social situations either. Our behavior is not necessarily dictated by the circumstances in which we find ourselves. Persons are active participants in these situations and can alter the circumstances and challenge the settings or those responsible for them. Behavior, therefore, is a complex interaction between ourselves and our circumstances.

Yet situational circumstances are powerful forces. Stanford University social psychologist Philip Zimbardo reports that a statistical analysis of 25,000 social-psychological studies conducted over 100 years and involving eight million people shows that situations are a significant force in shaping behavior.[58] Such evidence demonstrates that we can structure democratic procedures to reinforce good behavior and to get good results. That is why legislative juries are structured and run the way that they are.

For example, Zimbardo posits that prosocial behavior can be encouraged when there is "reciprocal altruism" present.[59] When a person thinks that others will respond to her as she wants them to, then that is how she responds to them. Mutual respect is thus reinforced, which is one of the qualities desirable in our democratic discussions and legislative juries. Zimbardo also points out that participants should engage in critical thinking, which is, of course, another vital aspect of democratic discussion.[60]

Perhaps most significant among the factors that Zimbardo introduces for promoting prosocial behavior is giving someone "an identity label." That is, you ascribe to a person the very characteristic that you want him to display. So if participants are encouraged to be open and responsive, then participants will display those characteristics consistently in the situation or, in our case, in democratic decision-making.[61]

Thus, the way that we structure democratic discussion influences how participants will behave in those discussions. If the rules state that participants are to be tolerant of views different from their own, if participants are to engage actively and openly with those different views, and if participants are to consider those different views seriously when reaching a decision, then participants will respond in this way. If the behavioral expectations are clear and the rules for meeting those expectations are also clear, then participants can and will meet those expectations by following the rules.

Consider, for example, the experiences of Peter MacLeod, the founder of the Canadian consulting firm Mass LBP. The firm organizes and convenes panels of citizens to deliberate on public policies related to their communities. Participants on the firm's panels are selected at random from those living in the affected communities. The panels meet with experts and policy decision-makers over several weekends. Topics have included subjects as focused as a local hospital budget to those as diffuse as mass transit. The key to the success of the panels—measured by the nuanced recommendations that the firm receives—lies, argues MacLeod, in the face-to-face deliberations of the groups. "If we design [deliberations] for participants' better angels, then lo and behold the phantom public that seems to haunt public discourse disappears."[62] That phantom public comprises political bystanders interested almost exclusively in the private pursuit of money and the incurious, intemperate, slogan-slobbering blowhards and dullards whom we often associate with public meetings, only because they tend to show up there. The open microphone is an invitation not to deliberate but to vent.

So the way in which we design democracy has a beneficial or pernicious effect based on what we demand that participants do. Deliberating with one another to come to a consensus on an important social or political issue and doing so through clear guidelines demands responsibility of participants. Social psychological studies and examples such as Mass LBP demonstrate that citizens rise to this challenge. But what of those few participants mentioned earlier who refuse to listen or to present their views, who wait only to vote for their preconceived positions? The key is to place such participants in a context or situation where it is difficult for them to behave in their usual way. In a democratic dialogue expectations are high that participants will share perspectives and will entertain

113

perspectives that oppose or challenge their own. As Zimbardo points out, a system that prizes critical thinking and deliberation prevents participants from sitting idly or, worse, from hijacking the entire process and preventing anything constructive from coming out of it.[63]

Constructing democratic decision-making in a particular way is therefore crucial to successful outcomes. The essence of our proposals for directly making rules and laws rests with deliberation, which assures that all participants have had a chance to offer their own positions and to challenge positions of others.

When all of those positions and challenges have been treated seriously, then participants consider the outcome of the process legitimate even if the outcome is not the option or policy that they themselves favor. Each participant feels that in the deliberative process she had an equal chance to affect the outcome or to win the day for her own position. Therefore, if the outcome goes against her own position, she can accept that outcome as legitimate. Nor is her autonomy diminished, for she has helped to make the decision and so has had a hand in making the rule, policy, or law that is to be put into effect, even if it was not her first choice.

Structures of Dialogue

Therefore, one way to structure direct deliberative democratic processes is to build in four elements:

a) an introductory phase of storytelling and trust building;
b) a phase of laying out participants' perspectives, ideals, questions, and concerns;
c) a phase of deliberating or reason-giving when policy options are explored and/or when perspectives, ideas, options, and concerns are critically examined; and,
d) an attempt to find a common policy, solution, or resolution based on or arising out of the perspectives and positions that remain after the deliberation phase (c).

As you can see, these four elements are conducive to participants sharing, hearing, and evaluating perspectives. The following example illustrates many of these elements of democratic dialogue. The example comes from Ms Gearhy's tenth-grade World History class in Newton, Massachusetts.

Three weeks after the September 11th attacks on the Pentagon and the World Trade Center, Ms Gearhy's 10th grade World History class postponed their lesson on ancient China and instead held a discussion on possible U.S. responses to terrorism. The discussion was based on the curriculum project Workable Peace, designed by the Consensus Building Institute.[38]

First, students were presented with four different perspectives on how the U. S. should respond to terrorism. All the students were asked to choose the perspective that most closely resembled their own positions. Then, based on their individual choices, the students were placed in one of four groups. Each group, representing one of the four perspectives, was to map out what it considered the most important elements that constituted their perspective. After these group discussions, the class reconvened to discuss together and to compare and contrast the perspectives from each group. Stacie Nicole Smith and David Fairman, representatives from the Consensus Building Institute, summarized the discussion in the following way:

> …[S]tudents not only defended their own deeply felt views but were also asked to listen to, restate, and acknowledge the needs and concerns underlying their classmates' perspectives. Rather than scoring points…the goal of this discussion was to develop a better understanding of how and why Americans might legitimately disagree on what the United States should do in response to September 11. Among the skills that the students practiced were explaining their views clearly, listening actively, acknowledging others' legitimate concerns, brainstorming options that reflected the needs of all points of view, and examining how the key issues might be resolved in

ways that would meet the primary needs and concerns
of others.[64]

All of these skills are important, if not central, to democratic
dialogue. Such skills help students address different perspectives
and process new knowledge. They help break down stereotypical
thinking and categories and, instead, highlight common interests,
values, and ideas. Missing from this example are two of the four
phases that we envision as vital for democratic dialogue in a
direct deliberative democracy. First, the students did not have a
storytelling phase, for the simple reason that they did not need
one. The storytelling phase allows participants to get to know
one another and to build trust and mutual respect. Knowing one
another already, the students did not need that phase.

The second phase missing in this student discussion is the final
phase. In our model of deliberative democracy the participants try
to come to some kind of agreement on a solution or resolution.
They try to find some way to accommodate the "primary needs and
concerns of others" by combining or transcending perspectives—
by "brainstorming options that reflected the needs of all points of
view," as Smith and Fairman express it—in order to find or build a
common solution. When those two missing phases are added, the
result is a form of deliberative, democratic dialogue.[65]

Also notice that at the outset the 10th graders were presented
with four perspectives from which to choose, which is the core
of the naming jury in legislative juries. A slight difference from
legislative juries is that the students in Ms. Gearhy's class divided
into four small groups. But this difference shows that different
groups, associations, or agencies can shape their democratic
dialogues in accordance with the different interests, needs, and
wishes of the participants or the issues they address.

In other words, there is not a formula for democratic dialogue
where "one size fits all." There is no blueprint to be precisely
duplicated or followed. Instead, we are presenting elements that
we think provide a sturdy foundation for democratic deliberation.
Ours is more of a framework, one for which we think the four

elements are essential. But creating democratic dialogues is an experiment. Nevertheless, the following describes the framework for desirable dialogue and lays out briefly why each element is for us foundational.

Phase One: <u>Storytelling</u>: Storytelling encourages each participant to say whatever he wants in whatever way he wants. Each participant, therefore, has the liberty to speak without fear of being interrupted, criticized, or challenged. Participants are not presenting cases or arguments; they are telling stories, stories about what happened to them or who they are. This is a way of introducing oneself to the group and, through personal testimonials, letting them know about one's experiences with the issue under discussion.

Storytelling also demands from participants a different kind of listening. Often when we listen to someone speaking, we immediately judge whether we agree or disagree. That judgment can color our hearing of what the speaker is saying. Storytelling, on the other hand, bypasses or undercuts such judgments. It is someone else's personal experience, whether the speaker's or another actor's, and so we can relax and simply listen. We don't feel the urgent need to filter what is said. This happens because we listen to stories emotionally, not just intellectually. We connect with the speaker, as we listen to the story with openness and at times with sympathy and empathy. This connection makes it more difficult to keep people at a distance. It is one way to bond and to build trust.

Phase Two: <u>Laying out Perspectives</u>: In this phase participants gather information. Whether that information comes from expert testimony, as in legislative juries, or from participants themselves, participants will hear multiple perspectives, questions, and concerns about the issue under discussion. In addition to information through testimony, whether personal or expert, participants are encouraged to explore other options, ideas, positions, and possibilities. Participants need the freedom

117

to explore and create options and ideas, even those that seem outlandish or on the fringe. These can spur new ways of thinking about or seeing the issue.

"Laying out perspectives" is for exploring, not criticizing. This phase is for brainstorming, "blue skying," speculating, imagining, dreaming. It is for generating ideas and options, not shutting any down. Daniel Yankelovich tells a story about the time in a steel mill when organized labor and management so distrusted one another that meetings to discuss downsizing the workforce resulted in name-calling and chair throwing. Finally, the owners of the mill brought in a mediator. At the first meeting, the mediator set no agenda. He simply told the participants to come up with rules for conducting the meetings. The participants did so, and because they had arrived together on the rules, both sides were committed to obeying them. Their deliberations led to both sides seeing the rules as legitimate.

In this instance, one rule that the mediator himself insisted on was having each side listen to the other side without issuing any criticisms or challenges or insulting comments. This took several meetings to achieve, mostly by letting participants just talk. Because this format of listening was so new for the participants, workers and managers alike, they had to spend time learning to listen without judgment. But their attentive listening shifted both their approaches and their attitudes. By the end of these preliminary "hearings," one worker commented, "You know, I can't tell who is on what side anymore."[66] Participants could then go on to offering new ideas on how to address the future of the steel mill.

Phase Three: <u>Deliberating on Multiple Perspectives</u>: Once a group of participants comes to know and trust one another, as they will do through phases one and two, it becomes easier for them to hear criticism of their own positions, perspectives, and ideas. In fact, once trust like this is built up, participants often find it a form of respect when someone takes the time to offer criticism.[67] The criticism means that someone has listened to the other perspectives and is taking them seriously. Of course, this show of respect then leads to participants sharing an even greater sense of trust, and that greater trust then makes it easier for participants to be open-minded about their own perspectives.

Where the second phase is about getting different perspectives out on the table, this phase is about examining and exploring the merits and consequences of those perspectives. The emphasis of this phase, then, is on deliberation. If deliberation is going to be fruitful, it needs to be on or about perspectives that differ. If participants do not hear different perspectives—and the more there are, the better—then they can fall into the trap of accepting pre-formed positions, those brought *to* the deliberation and not developed or refined or discovered *during* the deliberation. Cass Sunstein, for example, argues that the constitution of South Africa, which Sunstein calls "admirable," came about only because participants of one view were constantly hearing from people with opposing views.[68] The greater the diversity in the pool of perspectives, the better the deliberations go; the better the deliberations go, the better the outcome. Thus, phase two should provide just such diversity.

Listening to someone whose views are opposite yours, whose positions strike you as weak, even silly or dangerous, without any evidence or support, is difficult. We react strongly and immediately. Perhaps we do not say anything to that person; we are, after all, respecting the idea of tolerance, civility, and restraint. But we may very well stop listening. We have talked about the importance of listening, and listening to stories at the outset is one way to listen to someone's views and experiences without feeling a need to judge them. When someone is saying, "this is my experience; this happened to me," we are less likely to feel threatened or annoyed or angry. When the same person then offers some ideas about or reasons for a certain position, we might well refrain from judging, believing that we now know, as the saying goes, "where he or she is coming from."

A moderator can also play an important role here. As listening well is a skill, then how do we develop that skill? One

119

way is to adopt an attitude of curiosity about the views of other participants. Part of that curiosity comes through the first phase when we hear their stories and testimonials. Another part comes when we create new options and perspectives with them, when we brainstorm together. A third way is to have a moderator help us involve ourselves in the others' worldviews. She might ask, "How did you come to see things that way?" "Help us understand how you view this issue. What is your thinking process here?"

Because the focus of this phase is on deliberation, participants will challenge, defend, and modify the information generated through phases one and two. Deliberation is the method for probing and understanding the scope and nature of the viewpoints under consideration. By critically examining all of the options and perspectives before us, we can better understand what is behind those perspectives and what consequences follow from adopting any or all of them. Having deliberated, the participants are in an excellent position, then, to move onto phase four: making a decision.

Phase Four: Decision-Making: In this final phase participants attempt to build a consensus out of all of the options or action possibilities that they have heard and that have survived the deliberation process of the third phase. Consensus does not mean that every participant is enthusiastic about the decision or plan; it does not mean unanimity, as discussed in the prior chapter. It requires, however, that every participant can live with the decision or plan and thereby support putting it into action. All three phases are important to enable participants to get to this point, as they learn to work with and not against each other.

Daniel Yankelovich, the pollster and public-opinion analyst, commented through his own experiences with open dialogue that participants "often to their surprise...discover affinities with people with whom they strongly disagree. This experience transforms a battle...into a human encounter between people who feel a bond with one another even though their life experience has led them in different directions."[69] Conflict, therefore, in the right circumstances can be creative. In the circumstance of a deliberative dialogue conflict can be an opportunity to work together and to learn more about one's own perspective, as well as learn about those of others.

In such dialogues participants want to know not only that they have had adequate opportunities to speak, but also that they have been heard. This is part of the foundation of respect and trust operating within the early phases of the conversation. When every participant has had a turn and shared stories and perspectives, then there will be for the group an array of positions and perspectives. These may well clash, as in the three or four policy options resulting from the framing jury in legislative juries. Is it possible to find a consensus policy that combines some or all of these options, or must the group simply vote on the one(s) that they prefer? Either way, having been through the first three phases of the democratic dialogue, participants should be willing to accept the outcome, whatever it is. Even if conflicts cannot be resolved, at least participants have heard and expressed honest concerns and raised probing questions. They have heard and understood the positions of others and have heard and understood the concerns raised about their own positions.

Consider the example of affirmative action. Participants discussing this social policy may have differing, even divergent, views. Some see affirmative action as necessary for promoting justice, while others see it as unwarranted special treatment or pushing for racial quotas. Can these views be united by a common desire to pursue what is fair? In a debate setting, unlike a deliberative dialogue, advocates of the two different positions push their positions back-and-forth, and one side prevails, often to the detriment of the other side. By contrast, in a democratic dialogue participants build trust among themselves through stories and testimonials about their own experiences with affirmative action, about the positions that they hold and why they hold them. The purpose is not to score points, as in a debate. The purpose is, instead, to introduce a context for exploring the basis of and reasons for affirmative action, for examining the consequences of its different forms, and for raising and striving to answer questions and concerns about the policy, its scope, and its effects. Then, finally, it is to try to come to an agreement on how to modify the policy, or to implement it fairly, or to end its use, and so on.

The following is a fuller example of how deliberative dialogues can work. It comes from Mary Parker Follett, the early 20th-century American social worker, political activist, and democratic theorist.

All of the members of a farmers' cooperative association had agreed to market their crops through the association. The Executive Committee of the association discovered that a third of the members were not doing so, despite their established agreement. Some on the committee wanted to prosecute the offenders for violating the agreement; others thought that in many cases the circumstances facing the offending members explained and even excused their not living up to the agreement. Plus, it would have been costly and time-consuming to investigate every case.

So, after deliberation, the matter was resolved in the following way: No prosecution could proceed unless a local committee from the association had first investigated the circumstances. Follett comments that through such an investigation, both sides are satisfied: "One [side] because the policy of prosecution was to be continued; the other because the responsibility for prosecutions was placed in the hands of a local group."[70] The local committee that handled any individual case consisted of members who lived within the locale of the offender. Additionally, the cooperative membership overall saw this as an opportunity to create an educational program for the association. Not only did both sides participate, but they were also satisfied with the outcome.

The outcome was an integrative solution, rather than a mere compromise. A compromise more often than not leaves both sides with less, even if slightly less, than they wanted, but with enough to comply. In a compromise both sides give up something. But in Follett's example both sides got what they wanted. It was a consensus and an integration of the two opposing camps, because through the deliberations the group united on what was of value in each perspective. The outcome was truly a common good, something that satisfied both sides. Making a decision together facilitates acceptance of the decision. By considering multiple perspectives, especially opposing perspectives, participants can come to see their own views as partial or limited or incomplete. Working together enables participants to find what is valuable and true in the positions of others and helps them arrive at policies that might be more comprehensive, inclusive, or well-rounded.

If an inclusive or integrative solution is not found, then what? Well, a decision must still be made. One method for achieving a decision is to vote. Voting is not always a sign of defeat. It is a sign of disagreement among participants on the options available. As stated earlier, not everyone will agree with the outcome. But through an open, deliberative dialogue everyone can agree that the outcome, because it was made cooperatively and thus in good faith, is legitimate. There should be in the group sufficient trust and respect that the outcome of voting is a sign of a good decision, even of consensus. As described in the previous chapter on legislative juries, consensus is less rigid than requiring unanimity. But if a group cannot reach consensus and wants to call for a vote, there is an interesting variation to the notion of simple majority-rule voting that can be employed.

As a method for negotiating difficult labor problems, Cornell University's School of Industrial and Labor Relations (ILR) has developed a method called "Interest-based Negotiation," also known as "mutual gains bargaining" or "integrative bargaining." In this method the typical adversarial negotiation is reimagined as a joint problem-solving venture aimed at resolving each party's underlying issues, needs, and concerns. One of the first steps in the "IBN" methodology is to have all the participants voice any underlying history (or stories) that might affect the negotiations. By promoting this story-telling at the very beginning, the parties establish trust and create a basis for moving forward. After establishing ground rules and identifying the problems or issues to be resolved, the participants are encouraged to focus on interests rather than positions and to focus on integrative, imaginative solutions rather than "winning."

How does the IBN process focus on "interests" rather than "positions?" Consider the following: In most labor negotiations, the two parties come to the table ready to defend their "positions." For example, the "labor" representatives are interested in defending the position that they need higher pay. Management representatives, on the other hand, may be ready to defend their position that they cannot afford to offer higher pay. Entrenched in these adversarial positions, how can the two sides reach a compromise?

The IBN process, however, begins by having the participants focus on history first in the hope that some common ground may be found and trust may be established. Next in the process, participants are asked to focus on their "interests" and "concerns" rather than remaining entrenched in their positions. Yes, labor representatives are interested in higher pay, but by listening to the interests and concerns of the management representatives, the participants can turn their focus away from entrenchment in a position and toward imagining solutions that protect the interests and concerns raised by all the individual participants. A well-trained facilitator helps to keep the deliberations focused on interests and concerns, rather than positions, and in this way moves the deliberations toward jointly proposed solutions, not just compromises.

In this scenario, perhaps the solution that surfaces after all interests and concerns have been thoughtfully discussed might be to phase in higher pay as profits increase. This is not merely a compromise where one side gives up on higher pay or the other side gives in to higher pay. A solution was fashioned through the deliberations of all the participants. How is this agreement reached?

As the parties evaluate possible solutions, they engage in a modified form of "voting." In order to see how participants feel about a possible solution, instead of calling for a "yes" or "no" vote, each participant (all at the same time) indicates their acceptance or rejection of the solution by holding up a thumb. A "thumbs-up" means "I like this solution;" a "thumbs-sideways" means "I'm not crazy about this solution, but I can live with it;" a "thumbs-down" means "I can't live with this solution and we need to continue the deliberations." This is an alternative to the typical yes/no method of voting and could be quite useful in other democratic deliberative settings.[71]

A vote should be taken only after everyone who wants to voice a viewpoint has had an opportunity to do so, after those who speak have been listened to and heard to their satisfaction, and after everyone's perspective has been treated seriously throughout the phases. As a result, all participants can accept the outcome as fair and reasonable, especially when the outcome goes against their own positions or options. These points highlight what has gone into the deliberation and reinforce the idea that no outcome rests simply on the special status or standing of any participant or on any faction within the group.

This is especially important if the final outcome does not include an aspect of some participant's perspective or interest. The participant must feel that he had an equal opportunity to present his views for his position and even argue against those of others; he needs to feel that he has been heard. Then he can live with the outcome, knowing that he was honored within the group. But his perspective, although taken into account, did not make it into the solution...at least this time. "At least this time" is an important condition, because issues are not closed forever when a policy is made. Issues can be reopened when new information arises or when enough people want to revisit that policy decision.

Legislative Juries and Our Phases

All four phases presented here appear in "framing" legislative juries. There will be an introductory phase when participants tell their stories as they see fit, though sharing only experiences related to the topic under discussion would be most beneficial. This is followed by phase two or laying out the perspectives. In the case of the "naming" jury, however, and unlike the framing jury, the "perspectives" are already laid out in the sense that they have been reduced to or compounded into three or four alternatives. Of course, participants will have perspectives on the alternatives, some of which might well have come out initially during phase one. Phase two is also the stage for both juries when experts appear before the participants and give testimony in which they provide evidence and arguments for and against the options. Then, after the evidence has been presented, participants discuss that evidence. All participants should be satisfied that they have been able to share their views and that other participants have heard those views. At that point, the dialogue proceeds to phase three, the stage of active deliberation. Here participants challenge, modify, reiterate, and even transcend their positions. This is the phase of critique, when participants distinguish and identify strengths and weaknesses. That "identification" helps, then, with phase four, when the jury decides which option it favors.

What if the participants decide on an option that is not among the three or four from the framing jury? This is all the better, we think, *if* that option is a hybrid or compound of parts of the original three or four. That would be a consensus option that the participants had built out of all the available information, viewpoints, and policy options before them. Could there be a greater sign of success, of a successful deliberation? Of course, if a naming jury comes back with an option different from the choices produced by the framing jury, then a new framing jury needs to be convened, but this time that jury will have the additional insight of the naming jury that came up with a hybrid option or at least a different option. That is one way to proceed. Another is to form a different naming jury and add the new option to their list of possible choices. A third process might be to have multiple naming juries operating simultaneously, assess what these juries come up with, and if no others create the hybrid option, reconvene those same juries with this new option now available. As we prefer a process where more citizens are involved in the decision-making, then the multiple naming-juries process would be optimal.

CHAPTER SEVEN

Civic and Democratic Education

Before a jury trial can begin, the prosecuting and defense attorneys must select the jury from a pool of randomly chosen citizens. They do so after the process known as *voir dire*, from the Old French meaning "say that which is true." The attorneys have a chance through *voir dire* to exclude jurors who might be biased, either favoring or opposing their side before the evidence is presented. So jurors in a drunk-driving case might be excluded because they had a family member killed by a drunk driver or have themselves been arrested for driving drunk. Or perhaps a juror has professional experience in law enforcement, thus making it more likely that she might favor the prosecution. Or maybe a juror has a background similar to the defendant's and thus might have an emotional link to that defendant.

Whatever the range of reasons that attorneys might give for excluding a prospective juror, no attorney excludes a juror on the basis that that juror lacks the ability to deliberate. In fact, it is assumed that everyone in the jury pool is capable of deliberation.

Some might not be able to do so fairly in a particular case, which is why such jurors can be excluded. But that is not saying that a certain member lacks the capacity to deliberate on the evidence with other jurors. Quite the opposite. Our jury system is built on the idea that every citizen is capable of reflective thought and can use that thought in conversation with others when deliberating on the evidence.

For this reason, no one in the jury pool has to undergo any special training to deliberate on a jury. The judge delivers some special instructions in a particular case on how to apply the law, but the jurors use what are thought to be common skills when deliberating on the evidence and the law.

Although no one has to be educated in any special way to be a juror, there is good reason that children from an early age should be educated in deliberation. The reason is straightforward: for comfort. The more familiar children of all ages are with the deliberative process, regardless of the setting, the more comfortable they will be in engaging in that process. The more comfortable they are, the more relaxed they will be. The more relaxed they are, the more likely they will be to listen to others and to respond openly with their own stories, comments, and criticisms. For this reason, we would like to see our children, from elementary school through high school, educated in deliberation in settings we call "democratic schools."

Democratic Schools

Most kids do not spend nearly as much time or expend anywhere near the energy on their studies as they do playing sports, performing in plays, playing in the band, socializing with friends, getting food, and so on. Why not? Because most school work offers no tangible, immediate reward in the curriculum. This is why we take attendance and demand attention, even in college. It is not just that the work is often boring; it also seems to have little immediate pay-off. "How is what I am learning," a student might ask, "relevant to altering or improving my life right now?" This is also why teachers, at all levels, require schoolwork. Students won't do it on their own. Other than achieving a grade, they often do not see the relevance of the assignments.

But schools are real places, real environments, real communities...or can be. They can offer real experiences that have tangible results and that also have an educational component. That is, schools can and should be run democratically, where students of all ages, in conjunction with teachers and staff, make decisions that have an impact on the actual operations of the school and thus have a real impact on some parts of their lives in school.

As educators, we see that students learn best when lessons begin with or focus on real-life problems rather than abstractions. Schools that are run democratically—that is, democratic schools—use such real-life problems to prepare students to participate as citizens in direct deliberations and on legislative juries. Simply put, if we want students to be comfortable in deliberative democracy, then we need our schools to be examples, laboratories even, of deliberative democracies. If we want students to be comfortable with deliberations, then we must have students practice deliberation on real issues that have some effect on their immediate lives. This is not a radical idea. It was the cornerstone of the educational outlook of America's greatest educational philosopher, John Dewey. Dewey said that we gain knowledge of anything through experience and reflection on that experience. So if we want good decisions, then we need to practice reflective— that is, deliberative—decision-making. If we want knowledge of democracy, then we must experience democracy.

We cannot very well preach Dewey's philosophy to students and expect any results. But we can show them Dewey's philosophy in action by having them participate in deliberative democracy. Dewey wanted students to engage in "active inquiry and careful deliberation in the significant and vital problems" that confront the community, however the community is defined.[72] That is the essence of democratic schools—to ask questions about and to deliberate on significant and vital problems.

The community, in Dewey's mind, with which most students are concerned is the school itself. Dewey thought of schools as "embryo communities."[73] Schools are not quite like the communities that these students will live in as adults, but they have the feel of a community nonetheless. Children are members of schools, and those schools are the children's communities. Because children spend much of their day in school, we can think of it as a place where they live or are members as much as we think of it as a place where they learn. With the exception of sleeping they spend as much time in school during the school year as anywhere else. Therefore, it is not surprising that Dewey wanted to provide students with experience in making decisions that affect their lives in school. What is surprising, though, is that so little democracy actually takes place in schools and that those who spend so much time there have the least opportunity to experience it.

So, what constitutes a democratic school? To us, it is any school in which students engage in deliberative decision-making that controls some aspects of the functioning of the school or the classroom. The decision-making is not just a process for providing democratic experience. It is also a way for students to make actual collective decisions that affect some aspects of their life in school.

Of course, not everything in a school should be decided democratically. There are some areas in which decisions require expertise, which is not just experience but is experience combined with knowledge. Expertise rules out students as decision-makers in those areas. One area, for example, where students should not be making decisions is the overall curriculum. If teachers are to develop expertise, let alone be considered experts, then they must be involved in making the decisions most intimate to their profession. Teachers, in conjunction with administrators and with only minimal interference from school boards, should make decisions about the curriculum and pedagogical philosophy of their school. To deprive them of such decision-making not only undercuts or retards their exercise of autonomy, but also alienates them from what they do: teach. That they must defend their decisions before administrators and school boards is, of course, another matter.

We think that students should be left out of decision-making regarding curriculum for the same reason that members of the school board should be: Both groups lack the professional judgment, broadly defined, to make those decisions. Teachers are the experts on what students need to learn and how they need to learn it. Because the teachers and administrators in a particular school have firsthand and often intimate knowledge of the range and nature of their students' abilities and problems, as well as the particular circumstances in which the learning takes place, they should make the pedagogical decisions, not the school officials who are further removed.

Because many students are still children, the decisions that those children make should be age-appropriate. Not all democratic procedures or school issues are suitable for all ages. Differences in cognitive, social, and emotional development, especially at the elementary-school level, complicate open democracy. Educators must be sensitive, therefore, to the capacities of students at different levels.

It seems too much to expect, for example, children below sixth grade to engage in open deliberation with adults, which might be necessary in the democratic assembly (about which we shall say more later). There are solid developmental-psychological reasons for differentiating between the democratic procedures, as well as the topics for deliberation, used in high school and those used in elementary school. There is no general quarrel among developmental psychologists that all persons pass through three invariant states of increasing cognitive complexity. What most often characterizes these states, and accounts for movement from one state to the next, is the ability of persons to take up the perspectives of others.

Young children have difficulty taking up others' perspectives. On those grounds alone deliberative procedures that require the consideration of multiple perspectives would seem unsuitable for elementary-school children. Additionally, young children are far more reliant on the teacher's involvement in presenting problem situations in which the children can apply and develop their knowledge and skills.

For this reason, we imagine a hierarchy of democratic processes. The lowest level but the one that is central to all levels is the *democratic discussion*. It is democratic discussion that forms the basis of deliberative democracy and, of course, of legislative juries. Democratic discussion would constitute the entire direct deliberative democratic process for the lower grades, kindergarten through fifth grade.

The next level in the hierarchy consists of democratic discussion (Remember: It is the heart of all deliberative procedures.) plus the *democratic classroom*. This level is appropriate predominantly for middle school, approximately sixth grade through eighth grade.

The highest level of the hierarchy is designed with high-school students in mind. Students at this level continue to use democratic discussion, but since students in high school move from room to room based on the subjects that they are studying, the democratic classroom drops out. In its place is the *democratic assembly*.

We shall examine these levels in more detail, but before doing so, we need to issue a disclaimer. The democratic schools that we propose here are part of a larger program of civic education. Democratic schools, therefore, are an add-on; they are a supplement to other forms that civic education can and should take. So, for example, educators at the middle-school and high-school levels should make certain that within the social studies courses in particular, but spread throughout the curriculum in general, students should discuss, debate, argue about, ponder, and write about social issues such as justice, equality, tolerance, power, opportunity, democracy—grand topics and significant ones for society. But students should also devote some attention to issues related to their lives and their neighborhoods—issues such as teenage violence, teenage pregnancy, teenage suicide, gangs, drug use, unemployment.

Another aspect of civic education that schools can and should undertake is getting students out into their neighborhoods, undertaking projects that provide "service-learning" or "community engagement" and studying topics related to how well or poorly their neighborhoods function. Get students out into their local communities to explore the occupations, ways of life, and habits of residence found in those localities. Having students involved in the physical, historical, occupational, and economic conditions and circumstances of their communities is a way of conducting civic education.

Finally, schools should endeavor to have students learn about and participate in political action already extant in our democratic system. Beyond the obvious forms of voting, working on a campaign, or writing a letter to the editor of a newspaper, political action involves attending and participating in political meetings; organizing and running meetings, rallies, protests, fund drives; gathering signatures for bills, ballots, initiatives, recalls; serving without pay on elected and appointed local boards; starting or participating in political clubs; deliberating with fellow citizens about social and political issues central to their lives; and the like. If we include service-learning, as mentioned above, then we can broaden the concept of civic education even further to include various kinds of voluntarism and community work. Action here could include participation in the sphere of civil society, the network of non-governmental and private organizations differentiated from the family, the market, and the state. Students could be encouraged to volunteer at a soup kitchen, take part in a walkathon, clean up a neighborhood, organize a basketball tournament to benefit homeless children, or participate in and even lead other worthy causes. Such action exercises the skills that can be associated with political action. All of these are important kinds of civic education, which our schools sorely need.

But, now, to the elements in our democratic schools:

Democratic Discussions. The basis of classroom discussion is dialogue. Most often it consists of the teacher asking questions and the students responding. But the term "dialogue" comes from the ancient Greeks, for whom it meant a "talking through." In this case, the "talking through" would involve the teacher leading the dialogue, with a particular effort made to get students talking to one another; that is, getting students in a deliberation to talk through a topic, idea, or problem.

About what would elementary-school children deliberate? Discussions would focus predominantly on issues related to the curriculum—on stories, fables, or biographies; on science experiments, math problems, and historical events; on the students' writing; or current events. Discussions could even focus on aspects of the curriculum itself; how, the teacher might ask, should we study penguins, our next topic in science? How should we decide whose stories to read next week? But discussions should definitely include topics of interest to the children; for example, how should we celebrate classmates' birthdays?

In such discussions the teacher needs to model reflective thinking. He needs to seek out clarifications of positions or ideas, to ask for justifications for holding these positions or ideas. We know what these terms mean, and so do the teachers. The students just have to be asked to "say more" about their thinking. The teacher needs to summarize what students have said and to lead students from those statements to additional questions or illustrations. By doing so, the teacher models both reflective questioning and good listening. She listens carefully to what others say; she mirrors in her summaries what students have said; she looks for reasons and does not settle for mere opinions. Such discussions permit the teacher to respond immediately to what students say and allow her to recognize when a student is having trouble attending to the discussion or articulating a position.

Of course, because the students at this level are young and inexperienced, the dialogue is mostly between the teacher and students. Although student-to-student dialogue should to be encouraged, there must be strong teacher supervision and teacher feedback at this level. Students in these discussions need to see and to hear in order to learn what good deliberation is.

What is democratic about these classroom discussions? First, we should not expect children to follow the "structures of dialogue" discussed in Chapter Six, since those were designed for adults in legislative juries. Nevertheless, in democratic discussions, every child must be allowed to speak without being interrupted or harassed. Because the children are learning by doing, the teacher must be vigilant that important lessons related to democratic deliberation are in effect, even at this level. Therefore, the teacher may ask any student to summarize accurately what another student has said (or what the text says). This means that listening requires actually attending to the ideas of others. Although a student might have to translate those ideas into different words or ideas that make sense to her, she must learn to do so in a way that does not distort or misrepresent the perspective of the other student.

This is important for classroom discussions: Anyone who wants to speak can do so without fear of being interrupted and without concern that her ideas will go unheard or will be distorted. Speaking and being heard accord respect. Mutual respect is shown by the way that others hear our positions and thereby acknowledge us as persons and by the way in which we speak to or address others. Third-graders are not too young to experience and to learn that. The teacher must reinforce and enforce the rule of uninterrupted speaking and the rule of attentive listening. As students mature and move on to higher grades, the students will usually enforce such rules themselves.

One way to initiate elementary-school children into democratic dialogue—dialogue, that is, with one another—is to use the "circle meeting." Students' chairs are arranged in a circle, so that the children face one another. A discussion leader, who does not always have to be the teacher (especially as students become older and have more experience in democratic discussions), selects the first speaker. The next speaker is the student on the first speaker's immediate left (or right), and so on around the circle. Each person may speak for up to three minutes about a pre-arranged topic or, at other times, about anything related to that day in the classroom. No one may interrupt a speaker or comment while a student is speaking. The circle meeting involves all of the students, gives them equal time to voice their views, and elicits views from everyone. The point is to permit all students to voice perspectives knowing that no one will challenge them, that they can speak for three minutes or for ten seconds, and that there is no pressure to produce a right answer. This circle meeting is not unlike element two in the structure of dialogue in legislative juries—laying out participants' comments, questions, concerns, and the like. Children, even at young ages, have feelings and wants and viewpoints that they want and need to express. Among those "wants" and "needs" are the desires to be heard and to have one's views valued.

Democratic Classrooms. The purpose of democratic discussions at the elementary-school level is to engage students in the practices of giving voice to viewpoints, of hearing the viewpoints of others, and of questioning not only the teacher but also themselves. In the democratic classroom, however, the expectations should be higher for democratic discussion. For example, dialogue among students is expected; the teacher here is less the focal point. As with the prior level, students are expected to be able to articulate their own positions and to summarize other students' perspectives. But students are also to challenge others' positions and proposals. In short, they are expected to become the Socratic speakers and listeners that their teachers are in the democratic discussions in elementary classrooms at the prior level.

At the level of the democratic classroom real conversations take place, potentially with many more perspectives to keep in mind. More perspectives mean more complexity. That complexity can generate rapid intellectual growth among the participants. It certainly prepares students for the many perspectives that they are likely to encounter in legislative juries.

At this point, we have added to the discussion a level of in-depth and engaged conversation, part of which is being able to identify and challenge positions or ideas that are incomplete, shallow, or even untenable. So, the emphasis on respect continues as students learn to challenge respectfully. To do so students must first demonstrate, as at the earlier level, that they have accurately heard another's position. Only then can they offer criticisms of that position, criticisms based on reasons or evidence that the speaker did not present or maybe did not consider. The purpose of democratic discussion at this point, then, is not only to guarantee respectful challenges of different views, but also to structure constructive reflection and deliberation.

To assure that students take one another seriously—that is, to assure that they listen attentively to one another—Thomas Kasulis, Professor of philosophy at Ohio State University, uses the "listening-point circle" in his classes. This circle is different from the circle that we described for use in elementary-school democratic discussions. In the listening-point circle, "students may be called upon at any time to summarize what another student just said and to relate it to a previous point. Then the previous speaker explains whether the listener really got the point or not."[74] This technique is a variation, a sophisticated variation, of the one used in our elementary-school democratic discussions to see whether a student has been listening carefully. But Kasulis' technique also emphasizes that students speak with clarity. The immediate feedback from a listener, assuming that the listener was paying careful attention, leaves no doubt as to how well the original speaker has communicated her positions or arguments.

At this level the teacher leads the students through the elements in the democratic procedures to generate multiple perspectives. Then the students deliberate among themselves about turning those perspectives into multiple contributions that might lead the group to an acceptable solution or conclusion. Multiple perspectives can create a healthy tension that requires participants, including the teacher, to rethink and even to abandon a position. It seems likely that elementary-school students will not be able, or be expected, to recognize or to handle such tension, and so this level of democratic discussion is a development beyond those discussions held earlier.

Thus, at this next level, we have added another element from the "structures of dialogue" that we built for legislative juries. In addition to laying out perspectives, ideas, questions, and concerns, which happened at the elementary-school level as well, here we are adding the phase of critique, "when perspectives, ideas, options, and concerns are critically examined."[75]

What topics or problems will students deliberate about at this level? Remember: Students in middle school will continue to use democratic discussions. But those discussions might well involve problems that the students want, or are asked, to solve. So here the students themselves can generate the problems for discussion. Perhaps the most important issue for students at this level is how to manage and how to improve the classroom. Topics might include issues related to the organization, administration, activities, and operations of the classroom itself. To govern behavior in the classroom, the students might write their own constitution. They could begin by asking themselves, through a democratic discussion, what rules they think are necessary for their classroom. Does everyone have to obey rules? Why do we obey rules? What do we do when students disobey the rules?

We can see, then, that students' thinking about how to order their classroom has a real effect on their environment. Students want rules to live by, but they want more than simply to know what those rules are. They want a say in what those rules will be. Rules made by those who will live under them have a greater chance of being honored. Why? Because, as we have seen, those rules are recognized as legitimate. Even when people disagree with the rules that are adopted, they have some appreciation for the arguments behind those rules and for knowing through democratic discussion that their own ideas and arguments, while not accepted, were heard and addressed. This is nothing more than direct, deliberative democracy at work (or at school).

The crucial point here is that whatever the students decide must be acted upon. Thus, their constitution will govern classroom behavior and procedures. Rules made democratically are rules to be enforced and followed. Infractions will be punished. The exercise of creating a constitution must not be seen as an academic game or exercise.

In democratic classrooms it seems appropriate to break each class into smaller groups, groups of six or 12, like a jury. Small groups allow participants more airtime to articulate their perspectives and ideas and permit a sharper focus on the specific perspectives that arise. There is also less pressure to sound smart or to avoid sounding foolish. Small groups are often, even usually, relaxed and promote cooperation. Equally important, working in small groups prepares students for the small-group processes that are an integral part of the democratic procedures to be used in high school, as well as in the legislative juries themselves.

Democratic Assemblies. Schools are not just places to prepare students for careers and for citizenship. They are also sites of immediate political concern. Students want and need to address and to deliberate about rules and conflicts within schools, because these rules and conflicts affect the lives of everyone who inhabits those sites. Students at the high-school level are ready for such deliberation and decision-making. Are they really? Do they have the maturity—that is, the experience and judgment—to think through the possible intricacies of an issue? Can they identify key assumptions? Can they draw inferences and follow implications? Can they hear viewpoints with which they disagree? Can they accept the contributions of those whom they detest? Will they listen; will they speak; will they participate fully?

The quick answer to all of the questions listed above is "yes," provided that what the students are deliberating about makes a difference to them and that the issues are authentic and not just fictional exercises. Of course, we are still talking about school and the young adults within them. Participation is not voluntary; it is part of the curriculum.

But we cannot make people pay attention, listen carefully, or speak up when they don't want to. Because most of the issues will have direct bearing on their lives, most of the issues to be decided will appeal to the students. Such issues will involve how the school operates and how students can and must behave in it. For example, democratic assemblies might decide the time that school starts in the morning and ends in the afternoon; the lunch schedule; when the library should be open (on weekends?) and when, and whether, students should staff it; whether students should be responsible for policing the school premises; whether students should help maintain the grounds and buildings; whether an official student responsibility should be community service, such as coaching younger athletic or dramatic or debate teams; whether students should help prepare the cafeteria meals; what is offered on the lunch menus; how students dress; whether to have an open-campus; whom to invite to speak at the school during the year and at graduation; or what kind of prom to have and whether there should even be a prom.

Drugs are endemic in our nation's high schools. Is it time to draw the students into helping resolve the problem on their own campuses? What about problems of racism? sexism? violence on campus? Imagine that someone has defaced a school wall with obscene graffiti. This would not be a matter for the Discipline Committee, because no one has been caught or has confessed, and no rule exists covering such incidents. How might this matter be handled in a democratic school? Hold this example in mind while considering the following democratic procedures used to make collective decisions.

Democracy involves making group decisions, and therefore it makes sense to continue with the structures that we described in legislative juries. We have already considered how democratic discussions and democratic classrooms use some of these elements of dialogue. Those earlier structures served as the basis for learning and using dialogue and deliberation, but in limited contexts. So for democratic assemblies, we will continue by simply adding another element: the attempt to find three or four options for the democratic assembly to consider. This is the phase of the naming jury. Let us review each of these elements.

Stage 1: Laying out participants' perspectives. Since schools are designed with discrete classrooms to accommodate students, every classroom creates a Jeffersonian ward for deliberation. This means that every student will be assigned to a classroom or ward for the initial state of deliberation. The number of students should be in keeping with the homeroom concept: no more students than can be accommodated at one time in a homeroom—roughly no more than 35 to 40 students. Each ward is now a "framing" jury. Teachers will name their own 12-person framing juries, which meet simultaneously. Teachers not included on that jury will supervise, but not participate in, the classrooms, which are now student juries.

At this stage all participants can have their say. For example, participants can make contributions toward understanding or resolving the graffiti issue without fear of censure and without having their contributions subjected to criticism. To encourage such contributions, a school might propose having students initially meet within their wards or juries in small-group conferences and then convene as a jury to pool perspectives. If there is to be expert testimony during this stage, then that testimony should be delivered in a way that every student can hear and see. This might require an all-school assembly or the use of media, such as computer streaming.

However a school decides to implement this stage, it is vital that every person recognizes that the pooling is open to any and all contributions. Moderators of the wards, who may be teachers or even older students moderating younger juries, make sure that the process unfolds and moves along properly. Moderators have the power to ask participants, either before or after they have spoken, to summarize or to mirror the perspective of another. This is a way of ensuring that contributions are heard accurately.

The possibility that one might need to repeat another's perspective is important, because all perspectives, no matter how isolated or contentious, bizarre, offensive, or seemingly irrational, must be allowed to enter the discussion. Students at this stage are simply gathering perspectives as the database from which possible solutions, say, to the graffiti problem, will be drawn or on which possible resolutions will be based.

While not all perspectives will be included in the final solution or decision, since they will be scrutinized critically at the next stage, all must be allowed into the conversation and must be understood. The purpose of dialogue at this stage is understanding, not explanation or analysis. Participants are trying as best they can to understand the positions of others and are trying as best they can to articulate their own. Participants seek to gain some appreciation for the positions and situations of others.

It is illegitimate at this point to rule out any perspective. There is no sure way to know whether, and how, a flamboyant or offensive idea might affect the thinking of others. Such an idea might spark a conceptual breakthrough that transcends or incorporates divergent views. To dismiss out-of-hand certain views limits the possible options available to the jury, options that may not be readily visible unless all perspectives are pooled. At the same time, there is no sure way to discriminate between those views that should automatically be excluded and those that should automatically be admitted.

Stage 2: Scrutinizing Perspectives. Why should we "automatically" exclude or admit any particular view? Surely there are ways to assess perspectives, to challenge those that are obviously misguided, misinformed, incoherent, or irrational. Such challenges take place in this second stage, not the first. The second stage, the stage of scrutiny, is the time for critical analysis.

Contrary to debates, especially in politics, that are traditionally adversarial—in which predetermined positions are staked out and the purpose of any argument is to emphasize the weakness of the opponent's positions and the superiority of one's own—the key concept in this stage is exploration, exploring the nature, scope, and nuances of different positions. Participants must defend or criticize positions by using reasons and evidence; those holding views that are challenged are expected to make the best case for them. At this stage students will clearly demonstrate their critical thinking skills.

Yet participants will not be scrutinizing positions just to uncover weaknesses or contradictions and thereby dismiss them. Instead, participants are trying to find something in these positions that is beneficial or useful, something positive that might make up one of the jury's options.

As we suggested, the classroom or ward might divide into smaller groups, into small-group conferences. These smaller groups increase the possibility that more students will participate. Research shows that the smaller the group, the more likely that participants will speak, will focus on the topic, will follow the discussion, and will show initiative, cooperation, and an interest in influencing others and offering solutions. Smaller groups can be used, though they don't have to be, for the first two stages. But for the third stage, everyone in the classroom comes together to deliberate as one jury.

Stage 3: Generating Options. From the positions or perspectives that remain from all of the small-group conferences (if they are used) the students choose three or four options which retain them a variety of choices. The point is to find those options that capture the most perspectives and thus express participants' concerns and viewpoints. The students try to create a spectrum of possibilities, because once the three or four options are decided on, or framed—not by this ward or jury alone, but by all the juries in the school, including that of the teachers—then naming juries will render their "verdict" or decision from among the available options.

Of course, the options chosen should provide the naming jury with a variety of choices. Using our graffiti example, these options might include having students police the school grounds, designating one wall as a "graffiti wall" and even providing spray cans for ready use (maybe offering prizes for the best art), and living with the graffiti and having detention students repaint the wall after school or over the weekend. Whatever the jury decides, the options should reflect the disparate views of the participants.

When each ward or jury has completed its deliberations, then all of the options (obviously with multiple juries there will be many options) are brought to a central location where they are published and distributed to all students, staff, and faculty. Everyone then has one week to consider these options. After that week the entire democratic assembly meets as one group to finalize the three or four options about which the next juries, the naming juries, will deliberate. From those options the naming juries, again, meeting in classrooms, will select the one option on which their ward agrees.

Because the democratic assembly may not come to a consensus on which three or four options to present to the naming juries, then after a designated time for deliberation the assembly will vote. Those options that receive the most votes thus constitute the "ballot" that the naming juries will consider.

The naming juries deliberate first as small groups and then as one jury (per classroom). There is no need for stage one—laying out perspectives—since that step has already been completed. Nor is there a need for stage three—generating options. And so the purpose of the juries now is to select the one option that best expresses their collective judgment. When this cannot be done through consensus, a vote might have to be taken. In that case, the option receiving the most votes in a supermajority becomes the jury's "verdict." If there is no majority, then the jury deliberates until there is; a jury decision does not have to be unanimous.

We mentioned in Chapter Six the "thumbs up-thumbs down-thumbs sideways" voting procedure employed by Interest-Based Negotiation. The rationale for this process seems to be that voting itself simply indicates "winners" and "losers." In the "thumbs" process deliberations continue until all those who voted "thumbs down" have moved to "thumbs up" or "thumbs sideways." Clearly, there is merit in this procedure. Because the deliberative process conveys legitimacy when all participants have had a fair opportunity to offer their perspectives and to interrogate those of others, then it seems likely that a deliberative process will yield people either who agree with the outcome or who at least vote "thumbs sideways"—that is, are willing to live with the outcome.

Yet this might not always be true. It might certainly not be true in high school where a student's recalcitrance may be worn as a badge of esteem or could possibly be a new role for the student to explore. Under such a circumstance, that student might not yield under the weight of any evidence. The deliberation must then continue for, well, how long?

The quip about socialism attributed to Oscar Wilde now comes to mind: "The trouble with socialism is that it takes up too many evenings." So, some people might be willing to spend their evenings deliberating over issues until there is no one left to vote "thumbs down." But most folks want to move on from a stagnant issue to other more pressing or even more interesting concerns.

Additionally, there might be issues where on principle participants do not want to yield. Imagine that a committee proposes a new program that may offer great opportunities for students, but the money to finance this program must come from the arts budget. However, as is pointed out during deliberations, no such program has ever been tried before. Some assembly members, especially those in studio arts and in theater, might resist having money removed from the arts budget to finance a program with heretofore no proven results. No matter how long the assembly tables the deliberation—to be picked up next time, next assembly, next week—there is little likelihood of a different outcome. So should the new program be abandoned because some group of students will not vote "thumbs sideways" but continues to vote "thumbs down"?

Finally, the "thumbs" voting procedure *is* a kind of voting, where the goal is to get to a position where no one will vote "thumbs down." But what is wrong with voting "thumbs down"? Voting is not an indication of "winners" and "losers" any more or less than "thumbs sideways" is. A participant can always say of someone who votes "thumbs sideways," "You didn't get what you wanted; you only got what you can live with." Voting is a sign of preference, as is the "thumbs" method. The outcome to avoid through either procedure is to reduce the deliberation to "how did you vote?" rather than "what do you think?"

On the other hand, one of the merits of the "thumbs" voting procedure is that it brings every participant on board. Its efficacy, however, needs to be demonstrated. So we shall await the evidence from forums, large and small, whether local, regional, or national, for how well or poorly a "thumbs" voting procedure works on social and political issues. This version of our deliberative model is a supermajority model more than a consensus model. As stated earlier, we are offering a framework of direct deliberative democracy, not a blueprint.

So, having rendered its verdict, in this version of our model, through supermajority, each jury then sends its decision, once again, to the central location where the final tally of jury decisions is made. If there is a consensus winner, if one option is the overwhelming selection of the juries, then there is no need to proceed with more deliberations. The verdict is then officially announced. But if there is a close vote, a split decision, then the democratic assembly meets the following week to discuss as one group the two options in that split decision. At the end of the time period designated for deliberation, the entire assembly again votes on the options. Any option receiving a majority vote carries the day. That option then becomes the school's policy. The decision is binding.

Failure to secure approval by the majority of the assembly requires the democratic assembly to meet and to deliberate again. At this stage, for any option to become policy there must be support from two-thirds of the participants. In the graffiti example, the assembly might be considering two options, neither of which achieved a majority but far outdistanced the other two options. After the additional deliberations, the assembly passes a school-wide rule: anyone caught defacing school property must spend her/his free time over five consecutive Saturdays working on specific jobs related to maintenance of the grounds and the building(s). This option narrowly defeated the idea of creating a "graffiti wall."

146

Individuals who argued vociferously for the graffiti wall might be disappointed by and even disgruntled with the assembly's outcome. But they will still see that outcome as legitimate, provided they felt that their side had had a fair hearing—that their positions were well made, were heard, and were respected.

When to call a halt to the democratic process is itself a recommendation to be made by the wards through the democratic procedures, as is the ratification process itself. Some schools, for example, might want to extend the ratification process; some might want less or more than a two-thirds majority. Indeed, the democratic procedures should be discussed and decided by those in the schools themselves. Some might want no teachers serving as moderators in the students' wards, thinking that the students need to take responsibility for themselves. Others might want teachers to be participants on the student juries, with moderators picked by lot to serve for a specified time. In some schools teachers' wards could be the equivalent of the U. S. Senate to the students' U. S. House. Differences between what the teachers and the students want could be hammered out in a joint committee and then presented to the wards as a joint resolution. The Principal of the school might serve as the executive and hold veto power, which the House and Senate can override. Perhaps this makes the school board, then, the Supreme Court. Everyone in a democracy must learn to live with some disappointment.

3-D Politics: Direct Deliberative Democracy

However schools decide to implement democratic processes, they must be certain that the methods used are those that replicate the processes in which students will engage when they are adults. For us, that means that the schools must develop the skills of and create the settings for legislative juries. Schools do not have to focus the entire curriculum on an education in deliberation, since the skills associated with deliberation are ones that we assume all citizens have. But it cannot hurt to teach students the skills of critical thinking, which are essential to deliberation and which, surely, will give students confidence, and thus make them more comfortable, when they participate in legislative juries.

We bring this chapter to a close by quoting from *No Citizen Left Behind* by Meira Levinson.[76] This is to show just how prepared many students already are for deliberation, and yet how practice in deliberative settings can enhance their confidence and comfort. Levinson, now a professor at Harvard's Graduate School of Education, taught for eight years in two predominantly minority middle schools, one in Atlanta and one in Boston. McCormack School, her middle school in Dorchester, Massachusetts, was 90 percent minority students, with nearly 90 percent of those students qualifying for free lunches and with over half of the students themselves first or second-generation immigrants.

One spring Levinson arranged to have 30 of her McCormack eighth-grade American history students serve as jurors in mock trials argued by second and third-year law students from the Harvard Law School. Most of Levinson's students had never visited Harvard, though it was on the same subway line as McCormack, and few had ever met a Harvard student. But there they were, on a cold January day, in the federal courthouse in downtown Boston to serve as jurors in the Harvard mock trials. Here is Levinson's account of the outcome:

> …[M]y students settle enthusiastically into their role as jurors…As the trials progress, I wander from courtroom to courtroom, checking in on my charges…I am gratified to see each group ask, unprompted, for paper and pencil with which to take notes during the trial…I can't resist eavesdropping on three groups' deliberations…In all three cases, their deliberations are vociferous, with each student contributing something to the discussion. All of the groups take at least twenty minutes—and in one case, forty minutes—to review the evidence, develop a group consensus, and ensure that everyone is on board before they notify the judge of their verdict. After they deliver their verdict and the trial has ended,

each judge asks them to give feedback to the law students. As my students start to explain the reasons for their verdict, their analysis of the evidence, and their assessment of each lawyer's strengths and weaknesses, it is clear that the Harvard Law School students and the judges are initially taken aback and then awed by the depth of my students' thoughtful and sophisticated analysis. The law students admit to having been nervous about whether my students would understand what was going on, and to wondering whether they were really paying attention. At the end, they acknowledge that their fears were totally unfounded...[77]

Democratic assemblies and the levels prior to them are not, however, like mock trials. Beyond providing practice in and skills for democratic decision-making, which participation in mock trials does (as seen through the experiences of the McCormack eighth graders), democratic assemblies, democratic classrooms, and democratic discussions require students to make meaningful policies that affect part of their school life. As Ralph Waldo Emerson observed: Our democratic institutions are all educational; they require responsibility, and "responsibility educates fast."[78] Real issues for which students take responsibility will educate fast. These issues teach them, and us, something about our communities, our neighbors, and ourselves.

Consider, as a final example, the case of a permanent minority within a school. The example comes from Lani Guinier.[79] Imagine a school in which a White majority constantly overrules the Black students by outvoting the preferences of the African-American minority. The minority is outvoted on the music for the prom, on the kind of food they want served in the cafeteria, on the dress code. Would deliberation overcome the problem of this permanent minority?

Surely the process itself should make all students immediately aware of the problem, although increased awareness and sensitivity are no guarantee of redress. The hope is that through deliberation all students would come to see the problem in a wider context by asking themselves, "What kind of community are we creating and living in when some of us never get what we want?"

There are direct remedies for such a situation. On some decisions the faculty "Senate" might offer a counterproposal, or the Principal might veto a decision in order to move the students to reconsider the positions of the African-Americans. The school might experiment with a system of cumulative voting whereby each participant has multiple votes, all of which can be placed behind one preference, thus increasing the chances of victory if a bloc, say the African-American students, voted for one preference.

The point of any of these measures is to convey to all students the possibility of "asymmetrical intensity" on the issue, where an indifferent majority might overrule a passionate minority. In such a case, participants might proceed "with utmost caution," if not reconsider their decisions.

Such mechanisms may lessen the win/lose atmosphere that characterizes and plagues adversarial situations sullying much of our politics today, at all levels. Still, these mechanisms sidestep the central issue: Even within democratic deliberations some groups can continue to be at a disadvantage. One solution is to have the school create a "Student Bill of Rights." Another solution is to introduce this dilemma of permanent minorities as an issue itself for democratic deliberation. The school would deliberate directly on how to resolve the dilemma; then the whole school, that community, would be responsible for grappling with what to do on that issue. In this way, the conflict would be brought out into the open. Such a deliberation might well result in a Student Bill of Rights.

Conflict can be creative; it does not have to be destructive. Conflict can awaken us from our complacent slumber and shock us into seeing an issue in a wider context and from a different perspective. Conflict can bring us to a realization of different interests involved in a single issue, interests that must be taken into account if a solution is to be found. Conflicts about real-life school issues show in high relief that decisions made on these issues have an impact on the people who hold different positions. Real life school issues have effects on real people holding real positions that they find meaningful. Such issues teach all participants (faculty, staff, and students) how to behave responsibly in the face of real people holding deeply felt positions and how to decide responsibly when those decisions have real consequences for them. In other words, schools can be environments where community and politics meet and where members can practice democracy face-to-face. In democratic schools students practice the skills of deliberation, but not simply as rehearsal for performances later in their lives. Students are participating in real democratic decision-making.

Going to these lengths, creating democratic schools, may seem extreme given that this is a proposal made in the context of legislative juries and of direct deliberative democracy that do not yet even exist. It also may seem extreme in an educational climate in which teachers teach to standardized tests and in which many, perhaps most, people think that schools exist to prepare students for jobs. Yet, if we think that learning to listen attentively, speak carefully, cooperate with others, and assume responsibility for their decisions are worthwhile skills and attitudes for students as persons and as citizens, then we should applaud and push for just such democratic schools, in advance of changes to our democracy. We owe our children and our country no less.

Furthermore, if students learned these skills and experienced deliberative processes in schools, might they not clamor themselves for the kinds of democratic outlets and institutions where they could exercise their democratic skills? That is, perhaps they would demand the very kinds of democratic institutions that we are describing. Perhaps they would do so by putting into practice other parts of their civic education learned in school. People accustomed, as our students would be, to making direct decisions on issues important in their lives might not want to give up having that kind of impact. So they might demand of their elected officials and of other citizens more democratic outlets like legislative juries. To control, to author, to direct one's own life cannot be done by proxy. To be fully self-ruling we must be self-governing. The best place to begin that process is in our schools.

CONCLUSION

In *Federalist #10,* when Madison contrasts America's republic with what he calls "pure democracy," he has in mind such democratic schemes as those proposed by Jean-Jacques Rousseau. Rousseau argued for a direct democracy ("pure" in Madison's view) on the grounds that such a democracy was the only legitimate form of sovereignty for people who wished to be free. Yet Rousseau's "pure democracy" harkens back not to Athens but to Sparta. As we (now) know, both Athens and Sparta had democratic assemblies. But like those in Rousseau's assembly, citizens gathered in the Spartan assembly would not speak; they would only vote. Rousseau had something similar in mind when he said that citizens should vote their own individual consciences and not communicate with one another when they decide in the assembly whether a proposed bill or law is in the public interest. Of course, for both Sparta and Rousseau, individual conscience itself rested on an elaborate system of values education, including for Rousseau a plan for civil religion to promulgate the proper civic values. Otherwise, without such values or character education, neither Sparta nor Rousseau could be assured that citizens voting would get it right.

By contrast, in their assembly the Athenians had the right of free speech (*isegoria*). Any citizen could present his ideas to the gathered group. Athens, too, had an elaborate system of values education, which we might think kept the assembly from being simply a mob screaming for vengeance. Yet the Athenians were also careful to assure that the propositions put before the assembly were crafted in advance of coming before the people. In other words, the Athenians had a kind of representative democracy in the sense that a council (*boule*), representing a cross-section of the people, first met and framed the issue that came before the assembly for a vote.

So Madison might have been right to criticize "pure democracy" as direct democracy if he were thinking of Rousseau's democracy. But he was mistaken if he thought that such criticism also included the democracy of ancient Athens, because the Athenians showed just how a democracy could comprise both representative institutions and direct democracy. This is what we are proposing ourselves.

We are not suggesting an elaborate system of character education to try to instill in our citizens the "right" values. It would take another book to develop our ideas on that..[80] Instead, we are offering something perhaps even more effective: an emphasis on deliberation.

In addition, we are not arguing that all political power must be exercised by the people. Instead, we are arguing that the people themselves should exercise some political power and, perhaps more importantly, how the people should exercise that power when they do. Such exercise must be deliberative, and it must be so for two reasons.

The first reason comes from Aristotle. This might seem strange since Aristotle himself argued for what he called a "mixed constitution," one that was only partly democratic. But the democratic element had to be there, because, as Aristotle tells us, political decisions made through deliberation reflect a collective wisdom not found in any single individual's thinking, no matter how great or wise that single individual.[81]

The second reason comes from Plato, or his mouthpiece, Socrates. Most readers of the *Republic* will find Socrates to be a critic of democracy. But he is not an unalloyed critic; he also sees in democracy something unavailable in other types of regimes: freedom. What, Socrates asks his conversation companions, are the people in a democracy like? "Aren't they free?" he answers rhetorically. "And isn't the city full of freedom and freedom of speech?"[82] That freedom allows for the presence of multiple viewpoints, lifestyles, and ideas: "Then I suppose that it's most of all under [democracy] that one finds people of all varieties...This is the finest or most beautiful of the constitutions, for, like a coat embroidered with every kind of ornament, this city, embroidered with every kind of character type, would seem to be the most beautiful." A politics that brings that kind of multiplicity together when making public decisions will be a politics that most, if not all, people see as legitimate. So, too, as we have argued, is deliberative democracy.

Although we want to see "3-D" politics—direct deliberative democracy—we are not suggesting that every political decision must be made by the people. Rather, we think that many political decisions, those that affect our lives directly, should be made directly by the people. When the people make those decisions, then our exercise of political power should be direct, deliberative, and democratic. We are reticent to argue for wholesale democracy, where *all* decisions are direct, deliberative, and democratic, because we still think that there is a need for representative institutions. Certainly we need experts and representatives, for example, to negotiate international laws and treaties, free-trade and fair-trade agreements, and regulations of various sectors of the economy.

But we believe this country needs forums for direct deliberative democracy, lots of them, spread wide, spread everywhere. We want to see these forums in schools and workplaces, in unions and businesses, in law offices and hospitals, in corporations and PTAs, in NGOs and sports organizations. Above all, we would like to see real deliberation going on in state houses and Congress, on school boards and city councils, in every political office and agency.

Of course, deliberative democracy can take forms that look quite different from ours. We are merely suggesting one possible way of instituting it. We think that ours is a good way, but it is only one way. We are certain, however, that dialogue and discussion groups have demonstrably salutary effects on decision-making. In the United States, as far back as Kurt Lewin's studies immediately after World War II, social psychologists have shown again and again that dialogue in discussion groups can change, often dramatically, entrenched opinions and behaviors.[83]

Our view is that even small-scale deliberative and democratic settings can facilitate interacting with, listening to, arguing for, and integrating diverse, even contrary, perspectives. This is both empowering and a method for effecting good policy. Our hope is that repeated experiences with direct deliberative politics, at any level, will spur participants to put political pressure on larger organizations of which they are a part to enact direct democracy in those locations and venues as well. In this way we might build a bottom-up movement for direct democracy throughout regions, nations, and across the globe.

Can it happen that when a participant in a democratic dialogue addresses the other participants that she, as Emerson said, also addresses herself? It can happen through Tocqueville's "self-interest rightly understood," she can see that for some others her own interests are no different; and even when they are, it is possible to find commonality when everyone deliberates openly about them. This is the purpose of deliberative democracy. Every citizen is drawn into a conversation about how to achieve the public interest, the common good that serves all of us.

We don't have enough of these conversations, and we don't have enough of the kinds of forums necessary to host them.[84] Too few groups exist where people deliberate to make actual decisions, where participants do not just talk about important social and political issues, but actually create policies to affect those issues. Too few conversational dynamics exist where the diverse interests and perspectives of our multicultural society can be brought together, compared, argued for and against, and resolved.. Too often groups are isolated and focused on their own exclusive values and interests. Too often like-minded groups and individuals only hear from and only read the thoughts of similar like-minded groups and individuals. The ecumenism of the internet has not made this situation any better; indeed, in many ways it has made the situation worse. Groups and individuals are locked into their own self-interests with no way of making them rightly understood, and no impetus for doing so, either.[85]

Maybe the courts are such a place? After all, they often require jury deliberations. But courts are forums for adversarial debates, for winners and losers. We do not need more forums for talking *at* one another. We need places for talking *with* one another—places to tell our stories, to give testimonies, to hear testimonies, to discuss, converse, deliberate. We long for dialogue, not for more disputation.

What happens when we can't get out of our own special identity enclaves—our religion or hobby or occupation or the like? What happens when we meet only with folks who talk like us, look like us, and think like us? In such circumstances lost first are great national projects that could unite citizens, maybe something like a new kind of electrical grid or a new way of financing quality education. These are the kinds of topics that national initiatives could address. University of Texas Law Professor Sanford Levinson asked this question in a 2012 *New York Times* editorial: "Might we not be far better off to have a national referendum on 'Obamacare' instead of letting nine politically unaccountable judges decide?"[86] We think "yes," and we think, "Let's do it NOW," before more important decisions are lost to the unaccountable and the remote.

Lost next are virtually all effective forms of political action to go beyond just protesting what is being done. The Occupy Movement comes to mind—great potential but as of yet no political spearhead.

We have instead polarizing politics that consist of fights between one entrenched set of values and interests against another such set. In common parlance, which is about all that our current politics permits us to share, these are Republican politics versus Democratic politics. Can that politics unite us?

How can politics unite us? What do we want? As citizens and individuals, this is a central concern for us all, because how we answer the big questions will shape the kinds of lives we can live and want to live. Here we are not talking about the lives of isolated individuals, but our lives together. Seeing our individual lives in our collective life is not a matter of transformation, but only of recognition: What I want and need can sometimes be accomplished and understood only in the political context of what *we* want and need.

Direct deliberative democracy, even at the level that we are suggesting, threatens our representative republic. Critics of direct deliberative democracy, and let us count Madison among them (though who knows what he might think today), will say that direct democracy is torch-and-pitchfork democracy, rule by the mob; while deliberative democracy is only chatter democracy, rule by the verbose willing to waste too many evenings.

But as we have described and gone to some lengths to explain, direct deliberative politics is neither of those things. The real threat to our current politics is that direct deliberative democracy, especially among the children educated in democratic schools, would lead citizens to scrutinize campaign slogans, statements, and promises—things that were never intended to be scrutinized at all. It would lead thoughtful citizens to realize that many decisions in our nation can be and ought to be made by the citizens themselves. The first threat—the scrutiny of campaigns and political speeches—might make a politician look superficial or hypocritical, manipulative or wrong. But the second threat might actually draw power away from politicians and elites and bring it toward the people. That is where much political power belongs. It is democratic power, and it therefore belongs with the citizens. We should not be surprised that those who currently benefit from our democratic system have no reason to want to change the system. We should not be surprised, therefore, that they resist or even ignore any idea for such change.

Power can be distributed in two ways. First, it can be claimed or seized from the bottom through grassroots movements; second, it can be distributed from the top. We argue for both ways, though we prefer distribution from the top in the form of citizen-driven national initiatives rather than as begrudging concessions to grassroots movements by elites who prefer to drag their feet in response to the organizing of active citizens.. National initiatives might themselves have to be demanded from the democratic base through their exercises in micro-democracy, before the elites will move.

Demands for political power are sometimes characterized as populism, and they should be. But right now, and we should not be surprised by such a pre-emptive move, the Right has tried to seize the moniker "populist"—as in "Sarah Palin is a populist," a view propagated by Karl Rove and the Right after the 2008 Republican National Convention—to try to cozy up to "regular folks." Well, the Right has the right idea: Populism is about "regular folks." In the 2016 presidential election Donald Trump represented the anger of one part of the "regular folks" by speaking for the concerns of white, middle-aged, "poorly educated" (Trump's term) men who rallied to Trump's message of "Make America Great Again."

Populism has a history within the Republican Party, but it was not of a form that today's Republicans would like to accept. This is "prairie populism" that was about regular folks trying to break the stranglehold of moneyed interests. These early 20th century populists were after "radical" solutions, and they wanted to enlist government to break up trusts, increase corporate taxes, reign in lobbyists, and end government corruption. Today this populist movement to enlist government help is represented more fervently in the Democratic Party and was evident in the 2016 presidential campaign of Bernie Sanders.

Trump's populism was not fake, any more than Sanders' was. Both Trump and Sanders argued for "regular folks" by arguing against moneyed interests rigging the political system, against the loss of jobs through trade agreements and corporations moving jobs overseas, and against a healthcare system that is not good enough for the American people. Yet the constituencies that each candidate represented and the remedies that each proposed were stark contrasts. This can be explained, in part, by demographic shifts that enlarge the Democratic Party and frighten the Republican Party. The United States is changing. By 2060 no racial or ethnic group will have a majority. Given that Trump's demographic share is largely white and male, who constitute way less than 50 percent of the country, this news frightens his supporters. Meanwhile, this change benefits the Democratic Party where minorities have found a home. The demographic shift, therefore, led Trump to look to restore America's "greatness" by yearning for the past and led Sanders to plant hope for Americans by leaning toward the future.

Trump wants to make America great again by placing enormous tariffs on imports and penalizing US companies that seek to move operations overseas. He wants to prevent undocumented workers from entering the US and deport those who are already here. He wants to secure our country from terrorist attacks by banning further immigration by Muslims. Ironically, he can do all of this only by enlisting the resources of the federal government, the very institutions that he and his followers would like to shrink, if not dismantle. If you want to rid the coop of chickens, put the fox in charge of the henhouse.

Sanders also looks to use the resources of the federal government, but he does so because he values the role that government can play in improving the lives of our citizens. Sanders wants the government to offer free college tuition to anyone who wants it, to provide "medicare for all," and to break up the big banks. The government can do much of this by taxing the "millionaires and billionaires" who do not pay their fair share and whose financial lift-off has come at the expense of the middle and working classes of this country. As a "prairie populist" Sanders is not afraid to speak radically. Indeed, during his campaign he frequently called for a "political revolution." Unfortunately, his revolution amounted to little more than an earnest cry for citizens to turn out in large numbers to vote him into office and vote the rascals—mostly Republicans—out of Congress. He failed to take into account the astounding facts of incumbency reelection. Even populists who think the system is rigged and see Congressional representatives corrupted by money tend to believe that their own representative is just fine.

Both Trump and Sanders had populist messages, though from opposite ends of the political spectrum and with cures looking in opposite directions. Both also played within the system they both acknowledged is rigged. Trump's solution was to elect him to generate political change, because he is rich and thus not beholden to moneyed interests. Sanders' solution was to elect him to generate political change because he fights for the citizens and didn't take any campaign contributions from corporate donors. Never mind that neither had a detailed plan to end the influence of money in politics and governing. Moreover, both proclaimed the need to elect a strong leader, one who could stand up to big business and the politicians who reach into their pockets.

This is not the populism or the political revolution that we envision. We, too, deplore the elite control of our economy, education, military, and environment—the chokehold that corporations have on most of American life. The remedy for the decrease of oxygen to our brains—and we are not talking about hot air—is not just greater accountability from our elected officials or even getting better elected officials. That is a start, but it is tepid. Instead, we are talking about populism as a demand for greater democracy...for everyone. We want more deliberative and direct democracy for regular folks that can break the grip on our throats by the proponents, Left and Right, of "fat-catatocracy."

What is a good example of this populism? Instead of following both liberals and conservatives into the mosh pit of free-flowing taxpayers' money that Wall Street bankers currently play in, populists would, and do, growl for decentralizing monster banks into locally owned and controlled credit unions, cooperatives, and community banks. One could even argue for public banks (gasp!) like the state bank of North Dakota. All such banks have proven to be stable and efficient. Indeed, the Bank of North Dakota has had record profits for the past 12 years, with each year outperforming the previous year. Such banks can also be run directly and democratically.

So, on what level is direct deliberative democracy most effective? Where is it best for making important political decisions and for getting the attention of elected officials? Should we have small groups of citizens meeting throughout the country? Should we use the Internet and offer online dialogues? Should we have experts on podcasts, television, and online explaining different aspects of issues? Should we hold town-hall meetings and invite elected and appointed officials to present and to discuss their views with the public?

We should do all of these. Each suggests a different but important approach to holding dialogue. Small groups provide ample airtime for participants and encourage listening and trust among them. The Internet and the media are vital for people who are shut in or are unable to make small-group meetings. Experts are necessary for providing insights into and reasons for and against public policies. This is the basis of evidence for deliberations, though we would like to see citizens have an opportunity to cross-examine the experts. Finally, town-hall meetings enable constituents to hold their representatives and officials accountable. All of these, and doubtless other examples, are reflections of democratic dialogue. Part of the duty of the federal government ought to be to find ways to offer and to coordinate all such venues when discussing any national issue.

When participants hear different viewpoints on and stories about national issues, they learn what is tolerable and intolerable for each person, and why that is so. That kind of information, and the exchanges that bring it about, changes the relationships among the participants and can make possible policy choices that all can accept as legitimate. Indeed, it is a kind of emotional and persuasive storytelling that changes people's minds. Additionally, simply having to articulate why you hold the positions and preferences that you do can bring your own views into closer resonance with fellow participants.[87] During South Africa's National Peace Accord, for example, the dialogue between Afrikaners and the African National Congress—dialogue among all levels of the government and by persons outside of the government, as well as among the people themselves and with government officials—may be one principal reason that South Africa avoided a post-Apartheid bloodbath.

As we so often find, Tocqueville summarized our thinking in one pithy observation: ""It is really difficult to imagine how people who have entirely given up managing their own affairs could make a wise choice of those who are to do that for them. One should never expect a liberal, energetic, and wise government to originate in the votes of a people of servants..."[88]

We can manage our own affairs, because we can all deliberate. And by doing so, we can now not only imagine but also expect our government to be liberal (as in protecting our rights), energetic, and wise, because our government will then reflect the people who are its sovereign.

We hope that you now realize, having come this far with us, that one cannot simply put this book down and hope that someone else who has gotten this far will do something to further direct deliberative politics. That someone has to be you. It does not matter if you simply gather some friends together to discuss an issue important to you. That is a form of active citizenship, and it is a beginning; it is a start.

The Aztecs tell a story about a time when the earth was covered with forests. A huge forest fire started and quickly spread. All the animals tried to flee. As he fled, Tecolotl, the owl, saw a small bird flying back-and-forth from a nearby river and the fire. Tecolotl flew closer and saw that it was the Quetzal bird, who was filling his tiny beak with water and dropping it on the flames. Tecolotl scoffed at him. "You can't achieve anything by doing this. Are you stupid? Flee and save your life." The Quetzal bird replied,

"I'm doing the best I can with what I have." The Aztecs tell this story as the time the forests were saved from the great fire when a small bird, an owl, other animals, and people joined together to put out the flames.

Each bird, each person, does his share. At some juncture their work creates a critical mass, or a tipping point, that helps save the forest or saves the day or catalyzes action into a political transformation, internally or externally. We have seen the results of such "mass action" in Poland, in South Africa, in Burma, in Selma, Alabama.

Pressure from below can have monumental effects. Those who gather lack the political power to bring about major change; however, what those who gather do have is political will. It is a different kind or different expression of political power. Democratic dialogue can provide persons with processes and structures of deliberation and decision-making that can compensate for an absence of officially sanctioned political power. If the legitimacy of government derives from the will and consent of the people, and that will and consent are expressed through a dialogical outcome, then it seems difficult for government at any level, or the officials of any organization, to ignore that outcome. This is how political pressure can be built and then brought to bear. Through dialogue persons can generate political will and the relationships to coordinate, perpetuate, and grow that will.

So, begin your dialogue today; begin it now. Join in with or start today a group of friends, neighbors, co-workers to discuss important social and political issues. Then see where that takes you. Or organize a community or workplace or club deliberation on an issue important to those involved. Regardless of what you do, and at whatever level you do it, start today. Start now! Embody the democracy that you want to see.

Be the Quetzal bird, and do your part. From small movements, from intimate conversations, can come significant, even transformative, change. And you won't be alone. We guarantee it. Please join us by visiting our website at: www.3-dpolitics.com.[89]

NOTES

Introduction

[1] *Citizens United v. Federal Election Commission* is a Supreme Court case (2010) that permits corporations and unions to spend unlimited funds in sponsoring political ads that are made independently of any candidate's campaign. *McCutcheon v. Federal Election Commission* is another Supreme Court case (2014) that removed the limit ($123,200) that an individual can give to congressional campaigns each election cycle. While *McCutcheon* kept in place the maximum that an individual can give to any single candidate ($5,200) per two-year election cycle, individuals can now give that amount to any number of candidates, including every candidate each election cycle (in the amount, every two years, of $3.6 million).

[2] In 2009 alone lobbyists spent $3.5 billion on financing candidates, which amounts to $6.5 million per member of Congress.

Chapter One

[3] Hansen, Morgens Herman, *The Athenian Assembly*, Oxford: Basil Blackwell, Ltd., 1987, pp. 7-12. To be a citizen and attend the *ekklesia* one had to be a free male over the age of 18. Most historians estimate that there were about 40,000 citizens. Citizens were paid an average day's wage to attend the

Assembly and vote on legislation. See also, Finley, M. I., *Politics in the Ancient World*, Cambridge: Cambridge University Press, 1983, p. 34, and Barker, Ernest, *Greek Political Theory*, London: Metheun & Co. Ltd., 1960, pp. 38-40.

4   Aristotle, *Politics*, in McKeon, Richard (ed.) *The Basic Works of Aristotle*, New York: Random House, 1941, 1317b 20-1318b10. The numbers in the citations, instead of page numbers, are for Aristotle Bekker numbers and for Plato, Stephanus numbers. For an explanation of "Stephanus" numbers, please see Endnote 82, below.

5   Aristotle, *Nicomachean Ethics*, in McKeon, op. cit., 1107a.

6   Plato, *Republic*, in Cooper, John M. (ed.), *Plato: Complete Works*, Hackett Publishing Company, Inc., 1997, 563a. It is not uncommon in the present day for students to take legal action against their teachers, and there have been cases of children suing their parents. This has led teachers to fear their students and parents to be fearful of disciplining their children. There are numerous reports of students suing their teachers, but for a recent example see a news story at: http://abcnews.go.com/blogs/headlines/2012/07/calif-student-sues-teacher-district-over-c-grade/

7   The middle class in America does seem to be shrinking. See the NY Times article: http://www.nytimes.com/2011/11/16/us/middle-class-areas-shrink-as-income-gap-grows-report-finds.html?_r=0 This article cites a recent study from the Russell Sage Foundation American Communities Project of Brown University, *Growth in the Residential Segregation of Families by Income,1970-2009*, by Sean F. Reardon and Kendra Bischoff, Stanford University.

8   Hamilton, Alexander, Madison, James, and Jay, John, *The Federalist Papers*, Clinton Rossiter (ed.), New York: Penguin Books, 1961, p. 81.

9   Ibid., p. 81.

10 Ibid., p. 77.

11 Ibid., p. 77.

12 Ibid., p. 79.

13 See Kammen, Michael, *The Origins of the American Constitution*, New York: Penguin Books, 1986, p. 369.

Chapter Two

14 Two interesting and highly readable books on the founding are Stewart, David O., *The Summer of 1787*, New York: Simon & Schuster, 2008, and Beeman, Richard, *Plain, Honest Men: The Making of the American Constitution*, New York: Random House, 2010.

15 Even the ancient Greeks understood, as Aristotle observed, that human desires are insatiable and that those who enter political life, therefore, are often seeking financial and personal benefit. Aristotle, *Politics*, 1253a30-37, 1267b1-9, 1318b39-1319a1, 1323a36-38; see also the *Nichomachaean Ethics*, 1109a28-35.

16 The Founders, according to Edmund Morgan, "made no attempt to embody in the Constitution any manner of support for the traditional deference they apparently expected to see continued to men like themselves, well-to-do and well educated. They expected the national government they crafted in 1787 to be run by such people." See Morgan, Edmund S., *The Genuine Article*, New York: W. W. Norton, 2004, p. 43.

17 For a general discussion of egalitarian democracy in the United States, see Wiebe, Robert, *Self-Rule*, University of Chicago Press, 1995. For more on money defining fit character in the early republic, see Wood, Gordon, *The Radicalism of the American Revolution*, Alfred A. Knopf, 1992. Finally, for information about the self-interest of the first Congressional Representatives, see two articles: Wood, Gordon, "Knowledge, Power, and the First Congress" in Robinson, William H. and Wellborn, Clay H. (eds.), *Knowledge, Power, and Congress*, Washington, DC: Congressional Quarterly Press, 1991; and Rakove, Jack, "The Structure of Politics at the Accession of George Washington," in Beeman, Richard, Botein, Stephen, and Carter, Edward C. (eds.), *Beyond Confederation*, Durham, NC: the University of North Carolina Press, 1987.

18 Fearing the loss of states' rights and deploring the absence of the protection of individual rights, the Anti-Federalists opposed both the creation and the ratification of the Constitution.

19 Letter to William C. Jarvis, 28 September 1820, in Jefferson, Thomas, *The Writings of Thomas Jefferson*, Bergh, Albert Ellery (ed.), Washington, DC: Thomas Jefferson Memorial Association, 1905, volume 15, p. 278.

[20] For a more detailed discussion of, and for citations about, Jefferson's ward ideas, please see my book, Crittenden, Jack, *Democracy's Midwife: An Education in Deliberation*, Lanham, MD: Lexington Books, 2002, pp. 20-23.

[21] See Tocqueville, Alexis de, *Democracy in America*, Lawrence, George (trans.), NY: Anchor Books, 1969, p. 520, for the discussion of individualism and self-interest rightly understood.

[22] Ibid, p. 190.

[23] Ibid, p. 216.

[24] Kemmis, Daniel, *Community and the Politics of Place*, Norman, OK: University of Oklahoma Press, 1992.

[25] Ibid, pp. 70-71.

[26] Ibid, p. 71.

[27] Tocqueville, op. cit., p. 527.

Chapter Three

[28] Broder, David S., *Democracy Derailed*, New York: Harcourt, Inc., 2000, pp. 4-5.

[29] Ibid, p. 243.

[30] See Gerber, Elizabeth, *The Populist Paradox: Interest Group Influence and The Promise of Direct Legislation*, Princeton: Princeton University Press, 1999, p. 8. Gerber studied the relationship between initiative spending and interest groups and found that broad-based citizen support usually won out over money.

[31] Donovan, Todd, Bowler, Shaun, McCuan, David, and Fernandez, Ken, "Contending Players and Strategies" in Bowler, Shaun, Donovan, Todd, and Tolbert, Caroline J. (eds.), *Citizens as Legislators*, Columbus: Ohio State University Press, 1998, p. 84.

[32] Ibid, pp. 101-103.

[33] Magelby, David, *Direct Legislation: Voting on Ballot Propositions in the United States*, Baltimore: Johns Hopkins University Press, 1984; and Magelby, David, "Direct Legislation in the United States" in Butler, David and Ranney, Austin (eds.), *Referendums around the World*, Washington, DC: American Enterprise Institute, 1994.

[34] Broder, op. cit., p. 3.

[35] Ibid, p. 5.

[36] Ball, Terence, and Dagger, Richard, *Political Ideologies and the Democratic Ideal*, New York: Harper Collins, 1991, p. 33.

[37] Broder, op. cit., p. 241. Although Broder does not provide any evidence to support these claims, he is correct. For an overview of the major studies concerning the public views on politicians, see Kimball, David C. and Patterson, Samuel C., "Living Up to Expectations: Public Attitudes Toward Congress," *The Journal of Politics*, Vol. 59, No. 3, August 1997, pp. 701-728.

[38] Ibid., p. 3.

[39] Quite often initiatives are passed by the voters, but then fail to pass the required judicial review. In the state of California, for example, "only 26% of all initiatives filed have made it to the ballot and only 8% of those filed actually were adopted by the voters." See Waters, M. Dane, "*The Battle Over Citizen Lawmaking*, Durham: Carolina Academic Press, 2001, p. xv.

[40] Magleby, op. cit., p. 5.

[41] Magleby concludes that not only are voters ill-informed (by their own admission), but that they also are often confused by the wording of the ballot initiative. See Magleby's Chapter Seven, "Direct Legislation and Voter Rationality" in *Direct Legislation*, Baltimore: John Hopkins University Press, 2001, pp. 122-144.

Chapter Four

[42] Aristotle, op. cit., 1282a14-24.

[43] Machiavelli, Niccolo, *The Discourses*, Bondanella, Julia Conaway, and Bondandella, Peter (trans.), Oxford University Press, 1997, Book 1, chapter 58.

[44] For a sobering account that the Internet might not be all that democratic, see Hindman, Matt, *The Myth of Digital Democracy*, Princeton University Press, 2009. See also the article by Cass Sunstein, "The Law of Group Polarization," available online from the Social Science Research Network (http://papers. ssrn.com/sol3/papers.cfm?abstract_id=199668). In this article Sunstein argues that groups composed only of like-minded people reinforce their like-minded views and lead those with these views to hold them more extremely. The antidote to this is to create spaces or forums, as we've suggested, where divergent

views can be aired and heard. Indeed, the work of social psychologists, which we'll discuss in Chapter Six, show that in-group/out-group hostility can be reduced if not overcome by introducing cooperative ventures and procedures. See, for example, the work of Sherif and his colleagues in the 1950's at the Oklahoma boys' summer camp. Preaching to the boys about getting along did not work; only interactive cooperation among the boys changed their behaviors. See Sherif et al., *Intergroup Conflict and Cooperation: The Robbers Cave Experiment*, Norman, OK: University of Oklahoma Book Exchange, 1961.

Chapter Five

[45] The term "Legislative Juries" has copyright approval pending.

[46] Tocqueville, op. cit., p. 272.

[47] Kalven, Harry and Zeisel, Hans, *The American Jury*, Boston: Little, Brown, and Company, 1966.

[48] Ibid, p. 11.

[49] Taken from the *Discussion Guide* from "A Public Deliberation on The Coming of Age" sponsored by the Arizona Community College Association, St. Luke's Health Initiatives, National Issues Forums, 2002.

[50] According to the National Center for State Courts, "[F]rom 1980 to 1997, the total federal hung jury rate varies only 0.8 percent, from a low of 1.2 percent of all jury trials in 1985 and again in 1988, to a 17-year high of 2.0 percent in 1992." What is surprising about this data is the very low and stable rate and this is among courts *requiring unanimous decisions*. See Jonakait, Randolph N., *The American Jury System*, New Haven, CT: Yale University Press, 2003, pp. 99-100.

[51] More about Oregon's Citizen Initiative Review can be learned by visiting the website of Healthy Democracy Oregon at www. Healthydemocracy.org.

[52] Abramson, Jeffrey, *We, the Jury*, New York: Harper Collins Publishers, 1994, p. 8.

Chapter Six

[53] Chicago in 2009 was the first U. S. city to use participatory budgeting, in the city's 49th Ward. In 2011 four New York City

district councils used this process to allocate at least one million dollars each (with a total of five million dollars). Both Chicago and New York had help from The Participatory Budget Project (www.participatorybudgeting.org/). Currently some 1,200 cities worldwide use some kind of participatory budgeting, but at this point, no other major cities in the United States use this process. See www.worldbank.org.

[54] Mathews, David, *Politics for People*, Urbana, IL: University of Illinois Press, 1994, p. 187.

[55] Idem.

[56] Hamill, Pete, "Thrilling Show of People Power," *New York Daily News*, July 20, 2002, www.deliberative-democracy.net/resources/, accessed July 2009.

[57] Idem.

[58] See Zimbardo, Philip, *The Lucifer Effect*, New York: Random House, 2007, p. 323.

[59] Ibid., pp. 448-51.

[60] Ibid., p. 453.

[61] Ibid., p. 451.

[62] Worthen, Molly, "Where in the World Can We Find Hope?", *The New York Times*, The Sunday Review, February 19, 2017, p.9.

[63] Zimbardo, op. cit., p. 266.

[64] See two websites for the Consensus Building Institute: http://www.cbuilding.org/ and http://www.cbuilding.org/tools-workable-peace.

[65] Idem.

[66] Yankelovich, Daniel, *The Magic of Dialogue*, New York: Simon & Schuster, 1999.

[67] See Walsh, Katherine Cramer, *Talking About Politics*, Chicago: The University of Chicago Press, 2004.

[68] Sunstein, Cass, *Designing Democracy*, New York: Oxford University Press, 2001, p. 50.

[69] Yankelovich, op. cit., p. 105.

[70] Follett, Mary Parker, *Creative Experience*, New York: Peter Smith, 1951/1924, pp. 160-163.

[71] For more information on Interest-Based Negotiation, please visit the Cornell website at: https://www.ilr.cornell.edu/conflictRes/catalog/LR312.html

Chapter Seven

72 Dewey, John, *How We Think*, Buffalo, NY: Prometheus Books, 1991/1910, p. 55.

73 Dewey, John and Dewey, Evelyn, *Schools of Tomorrow*, New York: E. P. Dutton, 1915, p. 174.

74 Kasulis, Thomas, "Learning Philosophy as Plato Did—Not by Reading but by Conversing," *The Chronicle of Higher Education*, July 31, 1991, p. A32.

75 See Chapter Six, p. 103.

76 Levinson, Meira, *No Citizen Left Behind*, Cambridge, MA: Harvard University Press, 2012.

77 Ibid, p. 215.

78 Emerson, Ralph Waldo, "The Fortune of the Republic," *The Works of Ralph Waldo Emerson—Miscellanies and Natural History of Intellect*, Boston: Jefferson Press, 1911, p. 410.

79 See Guinier, Lani, *Tyranny of the Majority*, New York: Free Press, 1994, pp. 2, 14, and 72-73.

Conclusion

80 For more on this, see Crittenden, op. cit.

81 In his book psychologist Jonathan Haidt writes: "But if you put individuals together in the right way, such that some individuals can use their reasoning powers to disconfirm the claims of others, and all individuals feel some common bond or shared fate that allows them to interact civilly, you can create a group that ends up producing good reasoning as an emergent property of the social system." This insight, of course, should not now come as a surprise to readers of our book. See Haidt, Jonathan, *The Righteous Mind: Why Good People Are Divided by Politics and Religion*, New York: Pantheon Books/Random House, 2012, p. 68.

82 Plato, The *Republic*, 557b3-4. The quotations are from Plato's *Republic*. The numbers in our text that accompany Plato's quotations are Stephanus numbers. A French printer and classical scholar, known in Latin as Henricus Stephanus, divided all of Plato's dialogues into numbered sections, and then divided those sections further into equal sub-sections, each with its own letter, a-e. Stephanus numbers are therefore a convenient and universal system of reference for any of

Plato's dialogues. So regardless of what edition you pick up, you can easily find a passage or quotation by looking for the corresponding Stephanus number(s). Thus, our second quotation from Plato, on p. 231, is found in the *Republic* at Stephanus number 557c3-5.

[83] Lewin, Kurt, "Group Decision and Social Change," in G. E. Swanson, T. M. Newcomb, and E. L. Hartley (eds.), *Readings in Social Psychology*, NY: Henry Holt, 1952.

[84] While there aren't enough such forums and thus such conversations, the global trend might be in the right direction. "In Central and Eastern Europe, most of the 30 new national constitutions were enacted by national referendums...[and] the number of national referendums in the 1990s was more than triple the number of referendums in the 1980s: of the 405 national referendums worldwide between 1990 and 2000, 248 were held in Europe and more than 10% of these concerned questions around the European integration process." Please see http://democraciaparticipativa.net/documentos/DirectDemocracy.htm); visited on May 23, 2012.

[85] For more on this point about the Internet and democracy see Hindman, 2009, op. cit.

[86] See "Our Imbecilic Constitution," by Sanford Levinson, May 28, 2012, at http://campaignstops.blogs.nytimes.com/2012/05/28/our-imbecilic-constitution/?_r=0

[87] See "How to Move a Mind," by Koerth-Baker, Maggie, *The New York Times Sunday Magazine*, p. 14. In the article Koerth-Baker cites the work of Timothy Wilson from the University of Virginia who argues in his book *Redirect* that stories are more powerful than, say, social-science studies as means of changing people's minds and behavior. Stories, unlike such studies, allow individuals to identify emotionally with ideas and people, especially when they see those ideas and people as different from their own. Says Wilson: "Once you care about a character...you can find a way to fit them into *your* identity" (emphasis in the original, p. 15).

[88] Tocqueville, op. cit., p. 694.

[89] For a complete listing of all the books and articles that we have relied on to write this book, please check out an exhaustive bibliography located on our website at: www.3-dpolitics.com

BIBLIOGRAPHY

Abramson, Jeffrey. *We, the Jury*. New York: Harper Collins Publishers, 1994.

Aristotle. *The Politics*. New York: Cambridge University Press, 1996.

Aristotle. *The Basic Works of Aristotle*, ed. Richard McKeon. New York: Random House, 1941.

Ball, Terence and Richard Dagger. *Political Ideologies and the Democratic Ideal*. New York: Harper Collins Publishers, Inc., 1991.

Barker, Ernest. *Greek Political Theory*. London: Metheun & Co. Ltd., 1960.

Beeman, Richard. *Plain, Honest Men: The Making of the American Constitution*. New York: Random House, 2010.

Broder, David S. *Democracy Derailed: Initiative Campaigns and the Power of Money*. Harcourt, Inc., 2000.

Citizens United v. Federal Election Commission, 558 U. S. 310 (2010).

Crittenden, Jack. *Democracy's Midwife: An Education in Deliberation*. Lanham, MD: Lexington Books, 2002.

Dewey, John. *How We Think*. Buffalo, NY: Prometheus Books, 1991/1910.

Dewey, John and Dewey, Evelyn. *Schools of Tomorrow*. New York: E. P. Dutton, 1915.

Donovan, Todd and Bowler, Shaun. "Direct Democracy and Minority Rights: An Extension." *American Journal of Political Science*, Vol.42, No. 3, (1998).

Donovan, Todd, Bowler, Shaun, and Tolbert, Caroline J. (Eds.) *Citizens as Legislators*. Ohio State University, 1998.

Emerson, Ralph Waldo. "The Fortune of the Republic." *The Works of Ralph Waldo Emerson—Miscellanies and Natural History of Intellect*. Boston: Jefferson Press, 1911.

Finley, M.I. *Politics in the Ancient World*. Cambridge: Cambridge University Press, 1983.

Follett, Mary Parker. *Creative Experience*. New York: Peter Smith, 1951/1924.

Gerber, Elisabeth R. "Legislative response to the Threat of Popular Initiatives." *American Journal of Political Science*, Vol. 40, No. 1, (1996).

——————. *The Populist Paradox: Interest Group Influence and The Promise of Direct Legislation*. Princeton: Princeton University Press, 1999.

Gerber, Elisabeth, Arthur Lupia, Mathew D. McCubbins, and D. Roderick Kiewiet. *Stealing the Initiative: How State Government Responds to Direct Democracy*. Prentice-Hall, Inc., 2001.

Gilens, Martin and Page, Benjamin. "Testing Theories of American Politics: Elites, Interest Groups, and Average Citizens." *Perspectives in Politics*, Volume 12, no. 3, 564- 581, 2014.

Guinier, Lani. *Tyranny of the Majority*. New York: Free Press, 1994.

Haidt, Jonathan. *The Righteous Mind: Why Good People Are Divided by Politics and Religion*. New York: Pantheon Books/Random House, 2012.

Hamill, Pete. *New York Daily News*, July 20, 2002.

Hansen, Morgens Herman. *The Athenian Assembly*. Oxford: Basil Blackwell, Ltd., 1987.

Hindman, Matthew. *The Myth of Digital Democracy*. Princeton, NJ: Princeton University Press, 2009.

Jefferson, Thomas. *The Writings of Thomas Jefferson*. 20 volumes. Bergh, Albert Ellery (Ed.). Washington, DC: Thomas Jefferson Memorial Association, 1905.

Jonakait, Randolph N. *The American Jury System*. New Haven, CT: Yale University Press, 2003.

Kammen, Michael. *The Origins of the American Constitution*. New York: Penguin Books, 1986.

Kasulis, Thomas. "Learning Philosophy as Plato Did—Not by Reading but by Conversing." *The Chronicle of Higher Education*, July 31, 1991.

Kemmis, Daniel. *Community and the Politics of Place*. Norman, OK: University of Oklahoma Press, 1992.

Kimball, David C. and Samuel C. Patterson. "Living Up to Expectations: Public Attitudes Toward Congress." *The Journal of Politics*, Vol. 59, No. 3, (August 1997).

Koerth-Baker, Maggie. "How to Move a Mind." *The New York Times Sunday Magazine*, August 19, 2012.

Levinson, Meira. *No Citizen Left Behind*. Cambridge, MA: Harvard University Press, 2012.

Levinson, Sanford. "Our Imbecilic Constitution." *The New York Times*, May 28, 2012.

Lewin, Kurt. "Group Decision and Social Change." In G. E. Swanson, T. M. Newcomb, and E. L. Hartley (Eds.), *Readings in Social Psychology*. NY: Henry Holt, 1952.

Machiavelli, Niccolo. *The Discourses*. Bondanella, Julia Conaway, and Bondandella, Peter (Translators). New York: Oxford University Press, 1997.

Madison, James, Alexander Hamilton, and John Jay. *The Federalist Papers*. Clinton Rossiter, ed. Penguin Books, 1961.

Magleby, David B. *Direct Legislation Voting on Ballot Propositions in the United States*. The John Hopkins University Press, 1984.

——————. "Direct Legislation in the United States." In *Referendums around the World*. David Butler and Austin Ranney, eds. Washington, DC: American Enterprise Institute, 1994.

Mamet, David, screenwriter. *The Verdict*. Twentieth Century Fox. Sidney Lumet, Director. Fox-Zanuck /Brown Productions, 1982.

Mathews, David. *Politics for People*. Urbana, IL: University of Illinois Press, 1994.

Morgan, Edmund S. *The Genuine Article.* New York: W. W. Norton and Co., 2004.

National Issues Forums. Website online. www.nifi.org/ppiarticle. html. Internet. (October 2003).

NIF Moderator Guide for the forum entitled "By the People: Americans' Role in the World," November, 2002

Plato. *Plato: Complete Works,* Cooper, John M. (Ed). Hackett Publishing Company, Inc., 1997.

Rakove, Jack. "The Structure of Politics at the Accession of George Washington." In Beeman, Richard, Carter II, Edward C., and Botein, Stephen (Eds.) *Beyond Confederation.* Chapel Hill, NC: University of North Carolina Press, 1987.

Smith, Stacie Nicole and Fairman, David. "The Integration of Conflict Resolution into the High School Curriculum." In Noddings, Nel (Ed.) *Educating Citizens for Global Awareness.* New York: Teachers College Press, 2005.

Stewart, David O. *The Summer of 1787.* New York: Simon & Schuster, 2008.

Storing, Herbert J. and Dry, Murray (Eds.). *The Anti-Federalist: Writings by the Opponents of the Constitution* (abridged). Chicago: The University of Chicago Press, 1985.

Sunstein, Cass. *Designing Democracy.* New York: Oxford University Press, 2001.

——————. "The Law of Group Polarization." Available online from the Social Science Research Network (http://papers.ssrn.com/sol3/papers.cfm?abstract_id=199668).

Tocqueville, Alexis de. *Democracy in America.* Lawrence, George (Trans.) and Mayer, J. P. (Ed.). Garden City, NY: Doubleday/Anchor Books, 1969.

Walsh, Katherine Cramer. *Talking About Politics.* Chicago: The University of Chicago Press, 2004.

——————. *Talking About Race.* Chicago: The University of Chicago Press, 2007.

Waters, M. Dane. *The Battle Over Citizen Lawmaking.* Durham: Carolina Academic Press, 2001.

Wiebe, Robert. *Self-Rule.* Chicago: The University of Chicago Press, 1995.

Wood, Gordon. *The Radicalism of the American Revolution.* New York: Alfred A. Knopf, 1992.

_____. "Knowledge, Power, and the First Congress." In Robinson, William H. and Wellborn, Clay H. (Eds.), *Knowledge, Power, and Congress.* Thousand Oaks, CA: CQ Press, 1991.

Worthen, Molly. "Where in the World Can We Find Hope?" *The New York Times*, The Sunday Review, February 19, 2017.

Yankelovich, Daniel. *The Magic of Dialogue.* New York: Simon & Schuster, 1999.

Zimbardo, Philip. *The Lucifer Effect.* New York: Random House, 2007.